Also available from The Wisdom Library

The Wisdom of John Adams
The Wisdom of Jane Austen
The Wisdom of Buddha
The Wisdom of The Celts
The Wisdom of Confucius
The Wisdom of W.E.B. Dubois
The Wisdom of George Eliot
The Wisdom of Sigmund Freud
The Wisdom of Gandhi
The Wisdom of Gibran
The Wisdom of Thomas Jefferson
The Wisdom of Carl Jung
The Wisdom of The Kabbalah
The Wisdom of Omar Khayyam
The Wisdom of The Koran
The Wisdom of Mao
The Wisdom of Karl Marx
The Wisdom of Muhammad
The Wisdom of Eleanor Roosevelt
The Wisdom of Theodore Roosevelt
The Wisdom of Bertrand Russell
The Wisdom of The Saints
The Wisdom of Sartre
The Wisdom of Shakespeare
The Wisdom of The Talmud
The Wisdom of Thoreau
The Wisdom of Leo Tolstoy
The Wisdom of The Torah
The Wisdom of Mark Twain
The Wisdom of Oscar Wilde

Published by Citadel Press

THE WISDOM OF

The Celts

Edited by

Patricia King, Ph.D.
Gina Sigillito
Síle Deady

CITADEL PRESS
Kensington Publishing Corp.
www.kensingtonbooks.com

CITADEL PRESS BOOKS are published by

Kensington Publishing Corp.
850 Third Avenue
New York, NY 10022

First Wisdom Library printing: March 2004

10 9 8 7 6 5 4 3 2 1

Printed in the United States of America
Library of Congress Control Number: 2003107122
ISBN 0-8065-2530-4

Gina Sigillito wishes to thank her parents
and her siblings Séan, Bridget, and Michael

Editors' Note

Because of the various translations used in this book, spellings of character names will vary.

Contents

THE WISDOM OF
THE CELTS

Introduction

Patricia King

The Celts have always inspired curiosity and awe. From earliest times to the present day, very little is known about these elusive and mysterious people. To the early Greeks and Romans they were the foreigners living to the north beyond their borders. The Greeks called them *Keltoi* because they seemed hidden and strange; the Romans called them *Galli*. We do not know by what name these prehistoric Celts were known between themselves. Their learned leaders, Druids and *Filidh,* had a prohibition against writing. All their lore had to remain hidden, stored in the minds and hearts of the seers who formed the learned class. This closely guarded oral tradition was entrusted only to chosen initiates—to be learned by heart, pondered over in years of study and training in eloquence, and handed down from generation to generation to form a communal memory. What we do know about these ancient Celts comes to us in fragmentary form, culled from references in classical writings; from archeologists and linguistic scholars; and from the remnants of the tradition that were finally committed to writing by Irish monks, starting in the sixth century A.D.

When we consider how much of the Celtic past is missing or extinct, and the gaps in our knowledge of what we have left, we cannot but feel an enormous sense of absence and loss. The remnants that remain, splendid as they may be, are merely what the poet John Montague calls "shards of a lost tradition." Nevertheless, they are precious shards, like pieces of a stained glass window, which when reconstructed illuminates the past. The task of reconstruction sets us on a mythic quest across an ancient landscape in search of the grail that contains the wisdom of the Celts. We may never find intact this reliquary of the Celtic mind, but this makes us strive all the harder to follow the clues given in the traces we can find. The Greek and Roman writings are of some help in this quest, but we must remind ourselves that they were hostile witnesses; by the time they got close enough to the Celts to come up with any description, the Celts were a powerful adversary challenging Rome in its struggle for empire and world domination. The writings of the Christian monks retrieve only a fraction of the material, and they contain interpolations that demonstrate an ambiguous and conflicted attitude towards the pre-Christian past. As for archeology, only a small number of sites have so far been explored, and some of those explored have yet to be properly recorded. These sites are scattered all over Europe, and even farther afield, awaiting discovery and interpretation. In his long poem *The Rough Field*, itself a poetic field of force, drawing power from the past, Montague expresses this tantalizing truth:

> Scattered over the hills,
> tribal and placenames, uncultivated pearls.
> No rock or ruin, dun or dolmen
> But showed memory defying cruelty
> Through an image-encrusted name.
> . . . .
> The whole landscape a manuscript
> We had lost the skill to read,
> A part of our past disinherited;
> But fumbled like a blind man,
> Along the fingertips of instinct.[1]

1. John Montague, *The Rough Field* (North Carolina: Wake Forest University Press, 1989), p. 35.

As the technological aspect of archeological research improves, scholars are developing ever more exact tools for reading the landscape of the Celtic past. Since for the first millennium of their existence the Celts put nothing in writing, it is vitally important that we learn how to read and interpret the eloquent symbolism inscribed in the archeological and artistic heritage. By piecing together what we can glean from the evidence of archeology with the heroic narratives that began to be written down from the sixth century A.D., we get an awe-inspiring glimpse of a significant civilization underpinning the foundations of Europe, and foreshadowing in its social structure the kind of unity in diversity that constitutes the vision for the future of the expanding European Union.

It is generally agreed that the Continental Celts were first encountered in North Central Europe; the earliest archeological trace we find of their presence places them at the headwaters of the Danube, Rhine, and Rhône (rivers still to this day bearing their Celtic names). One of the first recorded mentions of these prehistoric peoples is by the Greek historian Herodotus, stating that the Danube has its source in the territory inhabited by the Celts. Linguistically this makes sense, since the Danube gets its name from the Celtic mother-goddess, Danu. Archeological exploration confirms this view; some of the earliest Celtic finds have been in late Bronze Age and Iron Age cemeteries in the area of Austria known as Hallstatt. This remote region was notable in ancient times for its rock-salt mines; salt was an important commodity in those days for preserving food, and along with iron, gold, and silver, provided these early Celtic peoples with a valuable trading edge and a growing prosperity. Since salt also effectively preserves organic remains, archeological exploration around the Hallstatt salt deposits has yielded valuable insights into Celtic life in the last millennium B.C. Because of these finds, the Celtic period from approximately 800–400 B.C. has become known as the Hallstatt Era. From the upper Danube region, the Iron Age Celts migrated and expanded their settlements until they occupied an area of Western Europe stretching from Gaul (France), to Iberia (Portugal and Spain). The Celts also migrated to Ireland and Britain in two waves—Goidels (Gaels) to Ireland and Brythons to Britain. The Celtic languages spoken by these insular Celts survive to this day among a small portion of the populations of these countries, in the form of modern Welsh, Irish, Scots Gaelic, and Breton. The languages spoken by the prehistoric Celts had a great deal of diversity, but enough in common to be recognizably Proto-Celtic, designated by linguists as an Indo-European language coming from the same source as Sanskrit, the classical language of the Hindus. From archeology as well as philology we find that the Celts made their first appearance in Western Europe at much the same time as similar migrations of peoples took place into India and Persia. The many similarities between the languages and worldviews of the Celts and the Hindus may suggest that both branch out from a common source in the prehistoric past somewhere in the steppes of Eurasia.

By the close of the fifth century B.C., the material life and culture of the Celts had become both prosperous and artistically sophisticated. Material evidence of this advance was uncovered on the banks of Lake Neuchâtel in Switzerland at a place called La Tène, hence becoming known as the La Tène period in Celtic civilization. These artifacts confirm the existence of a culture rich in acquisitions and resources, with an exquisite art and an extensive trade in luxurious commodities. La Tène Celts had by then expanded from their central base in Switzerland and southern Germany west into the Balkans, Transylvania, and Bohemia (the present day Czech Republic). They had also developed a network of trade routes within Europe and along the Mediterranean coast during this time. Gradually the multiple and diverse groups of early Celtic peoples, through migration or conquest, occupied large portions of Europe. Besides the *Boii,* and the *Insubres,* some of these early Celtic peoples were the *Bituriges,* the *Averni,* the *Aedui,* and the *Senones.* The *Helvetti* were a Celtic tribe settled in Switzerland and Gaul (the official name of Switzerland to the present day is Helvetia).

In fact, in the course of the last four centuries B.C., the Celts gave their names to many European cities and rivers. For example, London and Lyons are named for the Celtic god *Lugh,* Paris is named for the tribe known as the *Parisi,* Chartres for the *Carnutes,* and the Seine is named for the *Senones* (while its source is dedicated to the Celtic goddess *Sequana).* One Celtic group called the *Gesatae* settled as far east as Anatolia, Turkey, and named their area Galatia. These Galatians were the recipients of an epistle from St. Paul, the Christian apostle, and, according to St. Jerome, one of the fathers of the early Christian church still spoke a Celtic language in the fourth century A.D. During those last centuries B.C., Celtic languages were spoken and understood over quite an extensive area. Though many people still think of a Celtic heritage as confined to parts of England, Ireland, Scotland, and Wales, the reality is that the populations of France, Portugal, Spain, Belgium, the Netherlands, Germany, Austria, Switzerland, Slovenia, Croatia, Serbia, Bosnia, Hungary, the Czech Republic, Romania, Bulgaria, and even Turkey, and all of their diasporas, also have a share in the rich heritage of a Celtic past.

Around 400 B.C., probably because of pressure from population growth, large groups of Celtic peoples pushed south across the Alps into the valley of the river Po in northern Italy, settling and farming the fertile lands from Milan to Bologna between the Alps and the Apennines. The area around Milan had previously been settled by a Celtic people called the *Insubres* and named *Mediolanum*, later shortened to Milan; Bologna was named for the Celtic people called the *Boii* who also gave their name to Bohemia and to the River Boyne in Ireland. In time the Po Valley was named Cisalpine Gaul. The move south into Italy was made by way of the central Alpine passes and was motivated by the need to find more arable land for a growing and thriving population. These new arrivals were not strangers; earlier migrations of Celts had already settled in this fertile valley of northern Italy and had managed a peaceful coexistence with their Etruscan neighbors. However, when such vast numbers of Celts poured over the Alpine passes into their midst, the Etruscans felt pressured and called on the Romans for help. The Romans sent three envoys to check things out. This may have been the first face-to-face encounter ever recorded between the Romans and the Celts. According to the Roman historian Livy, the Celts were cool about the meeting, stating that they had never heard of these Romans but were willing to negotiate. This may have marked the first Roman exposure to the noted Celtic eloquence. In Celtic law, land was considered common property; the Celts felt that since the *Insubres*, a Celtic people, had been in residence prior to the new migration, they were not intruders and theirs was a rightful claim. When the envoys challenged this point of view, the Celts pronounced that they would win the land by combat. This outcome to the arbitration was not well received by the Roman ambassadors and one of them, Quintas Fabius, in a very undiplomatic rage, slew one of the Celtic princes. The Celts demanded justice according to their laws, asking that the family of Fabius be handed over until compensation was paid. The Roman Assembly not only refused, instead they promoted the murderer Fabius to the elevated post of Tribune. In retaliation for this blatant insult to their honor and sense of justice, the Celts marched south, and in 390 B.C. defeated the Roman armies at the Battle of Allia and laid siege to the

Imperial City of Rome. They did not come as raiders or marauders, but as proud warriors seeking revenge and vindication. After seven months of siege the Romans capitulated. The Celts agreed to abandon their attack in return for a tribute of one thousand pounds of gold. According to Pliny, the entire city was mobilized and hard put to come up with that much gold. The Celts then insisted on weighing the gold using their own weighting system. Again insulting Celtic honor, the Romans claimed this was cheating. In response the Celtic leader, Brennus, in righteous indignation flung his sword into the balance and proclaimed *Vae Victis,* "Woe to the Vanquished."[2]

Understandably, there was a fraught relationship between the Celts and the Romans from that time onwards. Celtic warriors were described with grudging admiration tinged with mocking hostility in classical Greek and Roman writings. Diodorous commented on their tallness of stature, their lime-spiked hair, and distinctive clothing: they wore: "shirts which have been dyed and embroidered in varied colors, and breeches which they call in their tongue *bracae.*" He also noticed the enigmatic nature of their utterances: "When they meet together they converse in few words and in riddles, hinting darkly at things for the most part and using one word when they mean another."[3] Strabo called the Celts "warmad," and noted their high-spirited sense of honor and loyalty: "On account of their trait of straightforwardness they easily come together in great numbers, because they always share in the vexation of those of their neighbors whom they think wronged."[4] Arrian described a meeting between Alexander the Great and a delegation of Celts. Alexander, having heard of their valor, "inquired what they most dreaded, hoping that they would confirm that they feared him above all else." Their answer took him by

2. Livy, *History of Rome,* V, 33, 48.
3. Diodorous, *Library of History,* V. 30.
4. Strabo, *Geography,* IV, 4.2.

surprise: "They said that their greatest dread was that the sky might fall upon them."[5] This may be an early recorded instance of subversive Celtic humor, or it may be an expression of wisdom as salutary fear, a cosmic awe based on a reverential sense of the precarious position of the human person in the universe. The Celts feared no man; they believed in living a brave and glorious life, however short it might prove to be, attuned to what the Irish hero Finn Mac Cumhail called the greatest music of all—"the music of what happens." This was life in harmony with the sacredness of nature, celebrating the recurring rhythm of the seasons with calendar customs, votive offerings, and festivals where tales of the glorious deeds of heroes were told—conferring them to an immortal memory.

The Celts of the later La Tène period developed ever more refined and distinctive art forms as they absorbed more and more influences from their travels. They brought to these art forms their complex worldview, their sense of divinity inherent in nature, and the strange shape-shifting capacity in things, suggesting alternate realities and mysterious communions. In the catalog accompanying the 1991 Venice exhibition "The Celts, the Origins of Europe," the curator Sabatino Moscati finds this distinction and originality of artistic vision remarkable: "We are without question in the presence of the oldest, the greatest, the most illuminating ornamental art Europe has ever known. It is the first instance in history of the great tension between illusion and reality, between the instinct to copy natural figures and the instinct to alter them in order to express meanings that are complex, symbolic, often rendered ambiguous under the very pressure of allusion, certainly surreal . . . all of which is very modern."[6]

5. Arrian, *Anabasis of Alexander* 1.4., 6-8.
6. Sabatino Moscati, et al, *The Celts, The Origins of Europe* (Milan: Bompieri, 1990), p. 680

In the last two centuries B.C., trade and cultural contacts continued to develop between the emerging European Celts on the continent and the insular Celts in Britain and Ireland. At that time France was called Transalpine Gaul, and it was populated by a variety of Celtic peoples. Rivers such as the Seine and the Rhône in Gaul, and the Rhine and Moseley in Germany and Switzerland were very important as trade routes. The Celtic peoples controlling these routes became more and more powerful and the commodities they controlled came under the covetous gaze of the Greeks and Romans, motivating their resolve to dominate and conquer. Within two hundred years, the proud Celtic warriors came to learn for themselves the anguish of defeat. By then the Romans—with characteristic calculation—had learned from the technological and military strengths of their worthy enemies, and carefully studied their vulnerabilities. At the battle of Telemon in 225 B.C., the Romans were the victors, and in 192 B.C. the *Boii* were vanquished at Bologna. The further conquest of the Celts in Britain and Gaul is memorably recorded in Julius Caesar's *Gallic War*. Caesar gives us a vivid account of the customs and battle strategies of the Celtic peoples, but we must remind ourselves that, however full of grudging admiration, this narrative is written from the point of view of the conqueror, justifying his destruction of a people and a way of life. Besides denigrating the Druids and distorting the religious beliefs of the Celts in his accounts of their practices, Caesar led a campaign concentrated on wiping out the sanctuaries and the intellectual and spiritual leadership of the Celtic peoples. In doing this, his aim was to obliterate the sacred sites and the oral memory store that preserved the Celtic sense of their own cultural identity and the difference in their mentality that made them resist his conquest.

The very essence of Celtic political thinking was the necessity to preserve autonomy and protect the sovereignty of the kingdom. Caesar notes his observation of this social structure: "There are only two classes of men who are of any account . . . the Druids and the knights. The Druids act as judges. If there is a dispute about an inheritance or a boundary they are the ones who give a verdict . . . on a fixed day each year they assemble in a consecrated place in the territory of the Carnutes; that area is supposed to be the center of the whole country of Gaul."[7] This center stood for the symbolic unity of the Celtic kingdoms. However, each *tuath*, or "people" conceived of itself as an independent microcosm, guardian of its own land, a bond and trust centered in a sacred place with its rightful king, its warriors, and its wise ones. There were many *Nemeton*—sacred sites, often at the sources of rivers or in sacred woods; hence there were many diverse Celtic kingdoms, jealously guarding their sacred boundaries, and frequently at war with each other. However, because they all shared similar belief systems, it was a restricted and neighborly kind of warfare, ritualized by custom, as recorded in the Irish epic *Táin Bó Cuailnge*, commonly known as *The Táin*. Caesar took advantage of this scattered nature of the Celtic kingdoms, and with his policy of "divide and conquer" he set brother against brother. In one memorable instance he befriended and made a collaborator of Divitiacus, leader of a prominent Gaulish people, the *Adui*. Dumnorix, brother to Diviaticus was the *Adui* magistrate or *vergobret*, vested with the sacred task of preserving the heritage of law and custom intact. Disagreeing with his brother's role as Roman collaborator, Dumnorix set out to create alliances with the *Helvetti* and the *Sequani* in order to resist Roman rule. Caesar had Dumnorix placed under observation and eventually assassinated. In her brilliant study, *The Celts*, Nora Chadwick notes: "The history of the two brothers is an epitome of the death struggle of a family and peoples under the ordeal of foreign invasion."[8] In 52 A.D., the Gauls made a final

7. Julius Caesar, *The Gallic War*, VI, 6, 13.
8. Nora Chadwick, *The Celts* (London: Penguin Books, 1997), p. 62.

heroic stand against Caesar at Alesia, but were defeated, and their brave leader Vercingetorix was led away in chains to be executed in Rome. Caesar went on to conquer Britain, making inroads as far north as Scotland. The Roman presence resulted culturally in a Romano-Celtic synthesis of architecture and beliefs. However, the Roman armies were frequently guilty of major atrocities. One notable instance was the pillaging of the East Anglian kingdom of the *Iceni*, on the death of its king. The queen, Boudicca, heroically resisted but was brutally flogged and her daughters raped. The outraged warrior queen united the armies of the neighboring kingdoms to avenge this offense to Celtic honor. In spite of Boudicca's fierce and courageous leadership, the Celtic Britons were defeated by the Romans under the command of Suetonius. The Roman conquest of Britain continued thereafter until the Fall of Rome in the fifth century A.D.

Ireland alone was left unmolested by the Romans, and because of its isolation was able to achieve a remarkable flowering of the La Tène civilization and art forms. This civilization continued to develop well into the Christian era. In many ways the Celtic gift for shape-shifting is exemplified in this seamless transformation of Celtic culture into a distinctive form of Christianity, characterized by the same love of nature and of learning. Recruits to the monastic life must have come from the ranks of the *Aos Dana*, the gifted artists and intelligentsia of the Celts. The leading learned families provided the bishops, abbots and abbesses, and scribes of the new dispensation. Great monastic settlements were a transformed version of the royal Celtic places of assembly—the head of the episcopate was situated at Armagh, close beside *Emain Macha*, the legendary gathering place of kings. The druidic sense of the sacredness of nature can be seen in the Celtic hermits whose love of nature's solitude led them to choose woods and streams, places long sacred in Celtic lore, as the sites for their dwellings. The vast store of knowledge to do with law, healing, and the sciences, as well as the epic tales of Celtic heroes, began to now be transferred to writing—the first time in Celtic memory. The Celtic cult of the head, which involved embalming the severed heads of heroes in cedar oil and placing them in intricately decorated boxes, was now transformed to include a "cult of the book": early manuscripts of Celtic books were preserved in specially made boxes, highly decorated with Celtic art patterns. The magical power of wisdom, once preserved only in the head, was now transferred to the book that preserved this power in the words and symbols inscribed on its pages. It is interesting in this regard to note that the early book called the *Cathach* is so called because it was the ritual custom to carry it three times around the assembled armies, in order to transfer on them its power before they went into battle. The famous *Book of Durrow* was discovered with its pages stuck together, because it had been customarily submerged in water so that the resulting healing properties of the water would cure the sick cattle of the land.

The learning that began to be recorded in the sixth century A.D. in the scriptoria of Ireland and Britain had already been preserved for more than a millennium in Celtic memory. Though the prehistoric Celts were not literate in the same sense as were the Greeks and Romans, they had a highly developed oral tradition, so excelling in learning and eloquence that they were frequently hired by Roman leaders to tutor their sons. The level of sophistication of their civilization is inscribed in the confident and understated subtlety of the artifacts uncovered by archeologists. With their excellence in metalwork and their remarkable skills in accessing and making use of iron in farming, in vehicles for transport, and in weaponry, the early Celts were more technologically advanced than their Greek and Roman neighbors to the south; and by their intricate international trading network, they played a large part in creating the first European common market. This hardly fits the picture of the languid and melancholy dreamers, later painted by writers like Ernest Renan, Matthew Arnold, and William Butler Yeats. The Celts who are the subject of these descriptions are the products of their authors' romantic fantasies, lost in a mystic mist, fading into a perpetual twilight. As part of his early version of an Irish Revival, Yeats made great use of the concept of a "Celtic Twilight." In *Finnegans Wake,* James Joyce mocks this mystique as "Cultic Toilette." The airy-fairy exoticizing approach to celticity is a persistent and perennial tendency not at all justified by reality. The Celts we encounter through historic accounts, through art and archeology, and later in the Welsh and Irish epics, are a very earthy people with a joyful and humorous wisdom, worldly and otherworldly at the same time.

The heroic narratives of Welsh, Scots, and Irish make up the oldest vernacular literature in Western Europe. Chadwick, commenting on one of its chief epics, points out its importance: *"The Táin* may be said to be the only European literature which gives us a picture of life in the Iron Age."[9] In *The Second Battle of Moytura,* a founding narrative of the Irish Celts, we find the names of the chief deities of their ancestors—the *Tuatha Dé Danann.* These are the people of the goddess Danu. Since the root "dan" means wisdom, the *Tuatha Dé Danann* may be described as the people of wisdom, which underlines how central this concept is to Celtic identity. The mother-goddesses are Danu, Brighid, and Boann. These are nurturing earth goddesses associated with sovereignty, artistic skill, and healing. The Dagda and Lugh are the chief male gods. The Dagda is called the "Lord of perfect knowledge," and Lugh is said to be multi-skilled, possessing mastery of all the arts. The Dagda brought with him to Ireland an all-satisfying cauldron, and a magic harp that plays the

9. *Ibid.* p. 270.

strains of sleep, grief, and laughter. The Badb and Morrigan are shape-shifting goddesses of battle, who often assume the form of ravens or hooded crows. The *Tuatha Dé Danann* arrived in Ireland led by their poet, Amairgin, who won the right of entry by chanting an incantation made up of eerie shape-shifting images: He declares himself a boar, a stag, a salmon, a hawk—all animals sacred to the Celts—and identifies himself as a Druid having magic powers. His song is similar to that of Taliesin, the Welsh bard, who, having gained magic powers from the cauldron of Cerridwyn, changes into many shapes to escape her wrath, and is finally reborn as a precocious little boy who declares himself "teacher of all intelligences, /able to instruct the whole universe,"[10] and grows to be one of the principal Welsh poets. There is so much emphasis on the magic power of wisdom in the literature of Britain and Ireland that Celtic society could be declared a wisocracy. The king must be wise, the Druids and Filidh must excel in wisdom, and a warrior had to acquire prowess in wisdom as well as weapons. Teaching this dual prowess was often the domain of women. Cuchulainn had to journey afar to a school run by woman warriors and wrest special knowledge and skill from Scathach and Aifè before assuming his role as champion of Ulster. The Welsh heroes Arthur and Peredur learn magic skills from witches at the Gwidon's Court. These special warrior skills increased heroic prestige—a person's "honor price" increased with his or her level of skill and knowledge.

Welsh literature was recorded later than the Irish, and is often influenced by later medieval notions of chivalry and Romance, but the stories of *The Mabinogion* and the poetry of *The Gododdin*

---

10. Cited in Joseph Campbell, *The Hero With a Thousand Faces* (New Jersey: Princeton University Press, 1973).

contain the same Celtic emphasis on generosity and valor; on the overlapping of natural and supernatural realms; and on heroic quests and vision tales. The Celtic god Llyr, *Manawydan* son of Llyr, Llyr's daughter Branwen, and Math son of Mathonwy are among the chief figures. The heroic Welsh tales continued to be recorded in manuscript form well into the Middle Ages. The Welsh material was popularized by Geoffrey of Monmouth, who focused on Arthur as the glorious symbol of heroism. The Arthurian material sparked a whole literature in many languages. Celtic influence on Dante's *Divine Comedy* stemmed from the visions of Heaven, Hell, and Purgatory recorded in Celtic voyage tales such as *The Voyage of Bran, The Vision of Adamnan* and *St. Patrick's Purgatory.* The influence of Celtic material can also be seen in Spenser's *Faerie Queene* and Shakespeare's *King Lear.* Over time, by dent of conquest, the Celtic-speaking peoples were pushed to the far fringes of Brittany, Ireland, Scotland, and Wales, learning the hard way the wisdom of endurance and survival while living life on the edge. Their precious traditions were hidden in monastic manuscripts scattered all over Europe and preserved in the folklore of the people, an oral tradition once again translated to far-flung lands by generations of emigrants.

Formal scholarly study of the Celts began with Edward Lluyd (1660–1709), a scholar at Oxford University and curator of the Ashmolean Museum. Through his linguistic and archeological work, Lluyd demonstrated the affinities between the Welsh, Irish, and European Celtic languages. German philologists continued this scholarship. During the Romantic Movement a new interest in faraway times and remote regions led to a further revival of interest in things Celtic. In 1760, the Scottish poet James Macpherson published what he claimed were fragments from the ancient poet Ossian. Though this work was indeed based on the Scots Gaelic version of the story of Finn and his *Fianna,* it was really a fabrication from the mind of Macpherson. Nevertheless, it won a wide readership and immense popularity; this Ossianic work was translated into several languages, influenced Herder and Goethe, and made a confirmed Celtophile of Napoleon. Serious Celtic studies continued in the work of the French Academie *Celtique*, founded in 1805. Its inaugural statement shows a Napoleonic eagerness to undo the work of the Roman conquest of Gaul and recover the remnants of the Celtic past: "To make up for the shortcoming of history, to turn new light on the darkness which covers the cradle of the Gauls." It describes this research as a work of service to the "French Empire, which by a series of glittering victories has retaken, and more, all the ancient extension of the Gauls."[11] In the same spirit of compensation for defeat and a renewed determination to recover the past, Napoleon III commissioned a statue of the Celtic warrior king Vercingetorix to be erected near Alesia, site of the Gaul's last battle against the Romans in 52 B.C. In a lighter vein, the same spirit of compensating for the defeats of the past can be seen in the creation of the Asterix comic, set in a fictional Breton Celtic village, never successfully conquered by the Romans. Asterix and his affable entourage embody the perennial spirit of resistance, so important in the history of France.

The influence of things Celtic is visible in the Arts and Crafts Movement of William Morris and Charles Rennie MacIntosh, and in the curvilinear style of Art Nouveau. Preoccupation with the material translated from Irish and Welsh by people like Charlotte Brooke, Lady Charlotte Guest, Sir Samuel Ferguson, and the scholars of the Royal Irish Academy sparked off the Celtic literary Revival in Britain and Ireland. This influence con-

---

11. Cited in Diarmuid Ó Giolláin, *Locating Irish Folklore* (Cork University Press, 2000), p. 40.

tinues into the present in a more popular form in the motifs of fantasy and science fiction. Writers as diverse as Robert Heinlein, Ursula Le Guin, Patricia Kennealy, and J. R. R. Tolkien make use of motifs such as the voyage Quest (transformed to the concept of "space faring" in Kennealy's *Keltiad)*, heroic struggles of knights and warriors with evil forces, the presence of wise mentors with magic powers, and the creation of alternative otherworlds—all recognizably of Celtic provenance. The perennial power of things Celtic is also seen in the wide appeal of the music of Enya, Clannad, De Danaan, The Chieftains, and the proliferation of computer games like Dungeons and Dragons, Myst, and Dune. Today we also see a strong revival of Celtic spirituality with its emphasis on a personal relationship with God and a deep sacramental love and reverence for the natural environment. The Celtic love of nature is also revived in the devotion of neo-Druids and eco-warriors, seeking an antidote to global consumerism; an alternative to living "amid the regimented cold inane," as Tolkien puts it in his "Mythopoeia."[12] These new Celts are bound together more by imagination than by ethnic origin; they are embarked on a shared quest for a more challenging and wise tradition within which to grow as individuals, and to protect and preserve nature and the planet for future generations. The wisdom of the Celts forms part of the myth-woven inheritance as described in Tolkien's poem: "endlessly combined / in living shapes that move from mind to mind."[13]

Celtic wisdom is an imaginative way of being in the world, and an inclusive manner of thought. In Celtic art and writing we find an absence of rationalist dualism—a non-oppositional way of thinking. The sacred and profane are not opposed but rather intertwined as inseparable aspects of the same reality. In fact, it

12. J.R.R. Tolkien, *Mythopoeia: Tree and Leaf* (London: Union Paperbacks, 1988), p. 51.
13. Ibid, p. 52.

would seem that the merely profane does not exist in the Celtic realm; all material things are charged with a dimension of the numinous, and epiphanies are about to occur at any moment, at any given occasion. The Irish writer James Joyce exemplifies this perceptual inheritance. In his aesthetic vision everything is capable of epiphany, which he defines as "a sudden spiritual manifestation,"[14] of its distinctive particularity. Epiphany is possible because of a capacity of our apprehensive faculty: any object can be perceived with clarity and led to reveal its inner radiance.[15] This epiphanic and metaphorical way of thinking is an alternative to matter-of-fact cause-and-effect thinking. As a way of perceiving reality, it seems consistent with what we have come to see as a Celtic view of the universe, not oppositional, not either/or, but rather both/and. The universe is celebrated in its ordinary particularity in Celtic art and literature, but at the same time its very ordinariness is seen to contain within it an extraordinary and marvelous dimension. Such a Celtic mind-set brings a more poetic approach to scholarship in the sciences with its focus on investigating the subjective aspects of learning and acquiring human self-knowledge, knowledge about nature, knowledge about what it is to be human, what it is to be the kind of person you are, and what makes each person different from anybody else.

This focus on what it is to be human and what constitutes individual difference is very timely indeed. Contemporary scientists as well as scholars in the humanities are currently engaged in a quest for more exact and profound genetic knowledge. Since the year 1990, the human genome project has set out to map and decode the genetic makeup of *homo sapiens*. The human genome is the name given to the total genetic material in a human cell. This is an exciting scientific project, expecting to be completed ahead

14. James Joyce, *Stephen Hero*, p. 211.
15. Ibid, p. 213.

of schedule sometime in the year 2003. The sense of amazement elicited by what has already been discovered is expressed in an Internet account published by the U.S. Department of Energy: "It is no overstatement to say that to decode our 30,000 genes in some fundamental way would be an epochal step toward unraveling the manifold mysteries of life"[16] It is fascinating to find out that there is such a close genetic bond between all of humanity, and that all our diversity can be traced back to about 30,000 genes. Humanity has developed so many languages and cultures— so much diversity—yet all are linked together by the strands and entwined spirals of our DNA. The Department of Energy statement finds this likeness in difference remarkable: " In a material sense, then, all the subtlety of our species, all of our art and science, is ultimately accounted for by a surprisingly small set of discrete genetic instructions. More surprising still, the difference between two unrelated individuals, between the man next door and Mozart, may reflect a mere handful of differences in their genomic recipes—perhaps one altered word in five hundred. We are far more alike than we are different. At the same time there is room for near infinite variety."[17]

Along with the focus on the material history of *homo sapiens*, it is important to explore the myriad cultural embodiments of the mental history of human development. *Sapiens* stems from the Latin word *sapientia,* meaning "wisdom." Think of all the amassed treasures contained in all the thoughts humans have ever thought, still floating out there in some sphere of reality waiting to be recovered. The accumulated wisdoms of human civilization, both eastern and western, are important sources for knowledge and understanding. Becoming wise requires that we keep growing and learning, remaining open to other perspectives and other interpre-

16. Department of Energy, Government Internet Publication, 11/25/2002.
17. Ibid.

tive frameworks. This openness of vision entails a journey toward holistic understanding and promises to launch us on the path to find the grail of harmony and self-fulfillment. Among the civilizations we will encounter on our quest for wisdom is that of the Celts. The wisdom of the Celts has a lot to tell us about the marvelous mysteries of life and the many modalities of our human consciousness. It forms a delicate but enduring tapestry whose strands are woven into a rich and complex pattern formed in the course of more than two millennia.

The wisdom of the Celts is like a deep underground spring: it is a source that slakes our thirst, and enables us to continue refreshed on our life's journey. Springs and wells and the sources of rivers have always been sacred places for the Celts. According to Nora Chadwick in her study of Celtic religion and mythology, "the source of all wisdom and knowledge is the well of Segais, at the source of the Boyne; those who ate of the hazelnuts which grew beside it, or drank the *imbas* (inspiration) from them became inspired with the seer's gift of poetry and prophecy."[18] The Celts had a vivid sense of the sacred immanent in nature, influencing their lives. The supernatural and the natural interpenetrate each other, and a calendar of ritual customs following the seasons mark this close communion. The main festivals—Samhain, Imbolc, Beltaine, and Lughnasa—all have to do with nature and the changing seasons, and are preoccupied at the same time with ritual devotion and votive offering to the deities. Samhain, celebrated at the start of November, is a festival marking the links between the living and the dead, the overlapping of worlds, the sacred time when a space opens up between the world of the here and now and the Otherworld, reminding us that we exist simultaneously on different planes of reality. This illustrates the value placed in Celtic lore on the wisdom of the sixth sense, an added

18. Chadwick, *op. cit.* p. 177.

dimension of mind, including a capacity to penetrate beyond frontiers, to think outside the box, conjuring up new visions, nurturing the kind of imaginative intellect capable of transformative leaps of logic needed to make generational advances in knowledge and invention.

The excerpts contained in this book allow us to share the hero's portion of the wisdom of the Celtic peoples; they take us on an Otherworld journey to discover what such diverse figures as Cuchulainn, Taliesin, the warriors of the Goddodin, Emer, Branwen, Rhiannon, Medb, and Finn Mac Cumhail, can reveal of the nature of honor, generosity, love, loyalty—all noble qualities celebrated in Celtic writings and transformed by the magic power of the Celtic imagination into marvelous mythic possibilities to which we can all aspire.

Chronology of Events

"The Cimbri devastated our lands and did us great harm, but in the end [they] leave our country and move on elsewhere. They left us our freedom, with our own laws and land. But what the Romans are after is quite different . . . they want . . . to settle on our land among our tribes, and bind us in slavery forever."

—The Celts, as reported by Caesar, on the indignity of having their liberty robbed from them after yet another invasion

750–450 B.C. Early Iron Age north of the Alps. The Celtic Hallstatt culture flourishes in the upper reaches of the Danube and Rhine rivers and their many tributaries. Their knowledge of ironworking would have been learned from the Greeks, who had acquired it around 1000 B.C. from the Hittites of central Anatolia (Turkey), where iron smelting first emerged about 1500 B.C. The main source of wealth of the Hallstatt Celts was salt, and it was their main commodity of exchange.

The long-established Bronze Age trade routes traversed Europe from the Atlantic to the Black Sea and beyond, and from the Baltic to the Mediterranean. The routes came together in the areas settled by the Hallstatt Celts, named after the site at which they were first identified in the mid-nineteenth century. The area of Hallstatt is in the Salzkammergut, or "salt mining area" of the Austrian Alps. The words *hal* and *sal* are synonymous with salt, and salt was at that time a valuable commodity worth its weight in gold—or perhaps, in this case, worth its weight in iron. Salt was essential for the preservation of meat, especially beef and pork, which were culled and cured in the late autumn, after fodder for livestock became scarce. This is when the Celtic festival of Samhain took place, at the end of the agricultural year, a custom that probably evolved in these alpine areas where the practice of *transhumance* (moving between mountains in summer and lowland valleys in winter) is still carried out. Even today, at the end of October, the cattle are brought down from the alpine pastures and are noisily paraded through the villages, bedecked with flowers and swinging and clanging their heavy bronze cowbells. The final ceremony is the removal of the bells and the ritual hanging of them on the walls of the barns, until the following May Day, when they are noisily released again. Not surprisingly, the agricultural calendar of the alpine areas follows the wisdom of the old Celtic calendar, though there is little awareness of this today. Ironically, the first of August is the Swiss national day, when bonfires are lit on the tops of mountains as part of an ancient tradition that must surely refer back to the Celtic harvest festival of Lughnasa.

The valuable resource of salt would have been traded for iron goods, such as weapons for combat and tools for farming. Knowledge of ironworking would have brought the Hallstatt Celts power, prestige, and wealth. This is evidenced by the rich grave-goods found in the early Hallstatt burial sites associated with the mines; they contained an array of weapons with iron blades, personal adornments and jewelry, and imported bronze vessels for food and wine. Luxury goods such as Baltic amber from the north and Etruscan wine flagons from the south, as well as oriental silks and elaborate bronze kraters from Magna Graecia in southern Italy furnished the princely tombs of the later Hallstatt Celts, whose chariot burials attest to a wealthy aristocracy of merchant princes, at a time when Rome was trying to wrest free of its Etruscan oppressors.

600 B.C.   Foundation of the Greek (Ionian) colony of Marseilles at the mouth of the Rhône.

500–50 B.C. Beginning of La Tène culture.

400 B.C.   Celtic expansion into northern Italy.

396 B.C.   Celts capture Melpum in the Po valley, northern Italy.

390–387 B.C. Celts attack the Etruscan city of Chuisi (in the Tuscan
                     Valley) under their leader, Brennus. Etruscans then seek
                     help from Rome, but the Celts defeat the Romans at the
                     Battle of Allia, twelve miles north of Rome. Famously, the
                     Celts subsequently sack Rome, the citadel on the Capitoline
                     Hill.

379 B.C.   Dionysius, the tyrant of Syracuse, employs the Celts under
                     Brennus to attack his enemies in Macedonia.

367 B.C.   Second siege of Rome by the Celts.

366 B.C.   Celts are recruited into Greek armies, i.e. the Spartan
                     Thebes war. Celts noted for their cavalry skills.

349 B.C.   Celtic raids as far south as Apulia in Italy. The practice of
                     single-handed combat, the practice of resolving conflict
                     by a form of fighting akin to dueling between two men (or
                     two women), recorded by Romans.

335 B.C.   Alexander the Great campaigns against the Celts along
                     the Danube River.

323 B.C.   Alexander the Great meets with Celtic emissaries at Baby-
                     lon, but they show little respect to him. When he inquires
                     as to why they show no fear, they reply that they "fear no
                     one or nothing, save that the sky should fall upon them."
                     Ironically, when they subsequently attack the treasury at
                     the temple of Delphi, an earthquake trembles the ground
                     beneath them and they flee in terror.

320 B.C.   Celts settle in the Carpathian Mountains, which border
                     Romania, Poland, and the Ukraine.

310 B.C.   Celts settle in the Ukraine.

300 B.C.   Celts establish strong base in southern and central Gaul (includes France and parts of Germany).

298 B.C.   Celtic invasion of Thrace (modern coastal Bulgaria) repulsed.

295 B.C.   Celtic Senones of eastern Italy are defeated at Sentinum (the ancient town of Umbria, East Central Italy). The newly founded Roman colony bears their name, Senegallia (near Urbino, Italy).

281 B.C.   Celts (Galatoi) defeat the Macedonians and kill their king, Ptolemy Ceraunos.

279 B.C.   Celts attack Delphi but are repulsed by another divine intervention—earthquake like that of 323 B.C.

278 B.C.   Galatoi serve as mercenaries to King Nicomedes of Bithynia in Anatolia and settle there (NW Turkey along Black Sea). That same year they found the "Robber Kingdom" of Tylis, also on the Black Sea (in Thrace).

274 B.C.   Ptolemy I of Egypt recruits Celtic soldiers, who try to loot the treasury of Alexandria, and are severely punished. There is a sculpted head of a Celt in the museum of Cairo, all that is left of a monument celebrating the defeat of the Celts in Egypt.

240 B.C.   Galatians of Asia Minor attack King Attalos I of Pergamum (Turkey). They sack the temple of Apollo but are repulsed and defeated at the Springs of Caicus. The Pergamese erect a large life-size group of bronze figures celebrating their victory over the Celts. (The famous dying Gaul in the Capital Museum in Rome is a marble copy of the central figure, while the other famous figure is the statue of Gaul killing his wife, found today in the Palazzo Attemps, in Rome.) This sculpture shows the respect that the Pergamese had for their enemies, as it hon-

ors their bravery and fearlessness in battle. It also reflects what the classical writers tell us about the fearless, almost foolhardy practice of rushing into battle naked with lime-slaked hair standing stiffly and raked backwards. The Greeks believed that the Celts were descendants of amazons and titans (the Greek word for lime white is "titanium,") and because of this they may have regarded them as their equals.

237 B.C.   In Spain the Carthaginians (from Carthage, North Africa) begin to encroach on Celtiberian territory to the north.

225 B.C.   Battle of Telamon, Italy. Romans inflict a major defeat on the Celts. Over the next few years there are various Roman campaigns against the Celts in Cisalpine Gaul (Cisalpine meaning "on this side of the Alps"). For the first time in recorded history the Germanic people are mentioned by the classical writers as fighting alongside the Celts as mercenaries. The battle of Clastidium (near Alba, Italy) was another major defeat for the Celts during which their leader, Britomaros, was killed in single-handed combat with the Roman commander Marcellus. Single-handed combat was a Celtic method of fighting, as we know from the story of Finn and Cuchulainn. It was a practice the Celts often used to determine the outcome of a battle. The Romans eventually outlawed the practice as it was becoming acceptable within its army and was costing them dearly. However, their worries were soon over as the Celts were eventually squeezed out by the Romans from the south and the Germanic hordes pressing down from the north.

221–218 B.C. Back in Spain, Hamilcar, the brother of Hannibal and the conquerer of Celtic territories, assassinated by a Celt. Hannibal takes over the further conquest of Spain and recruits Celtiberians into his army. His plan is to wage war on Rome using Celtic allies in Gaul to help him on his long, arduous journey over the Alps. Some Celts (such as the Tectosages of Gaul) try to thwart him as he crosses the Rhône, but they are defeated. A total of ten thousand Celts join his army in the hope of reversing their losses to the advances of Roman expansion. Over the next ten years the Second Punic War is fought with victories and losses on both sides. Hannibal returns to Carthage to defend his empire.

201B.C.   The Battle of Zama was Hannibal's last battle in which the Celts held a central position in his battle line. The great Roman general, Gaius Scipio, inflicted the final defeat on the Carthaginians and Celts in Spain. Back in Italy, Rome begins the conquest of Cisalpine Gaul, with the defeat of the Cenomani (197 B.C.). The next Celtic tribe under threat were the Boii, after whom the city of Bologna is named. Their chief and his family surrender to Rome but are slain for entertainment. Bononia (Bologna), the last Italian stronghold, is seized. The remaining Boii flee northwards over the Alps, some to Bohemia (which is also named after them and from which their ancestors had originally come). In the Museum of Prague there is a famous Celtic head found in a sacred enclosure at Msecke Zehrovice. It wears a torque and moustache and its hair is severely combed back in the fearsome manner described in literary sources. It is almost two hundred years since the Celts first sacked Rome.

Back in Asia Minor, the Greeks of Pergamum have inflicted more defeats on the Celts of Galatia, who are known as the Tolistoboii (232 B.C.). Some years later, Attalos of Pergamum recruits European Celts (Aegosages) into his army. These Celts are later massacred by Prusias I of Bithynia on the Black Sea. Sometime later, the Celtic kingdom of Thylos Thrace, also on the Black Sea, loses its Celtic identity. Elsewhere in Egypt, fourteen thousand Celts make up the major part of Ptolemy IV army in Egypt during his successful battles against Antiochus II of Syria (217 B.C.). The mercenary nature of the Celts is seen in the way they align themselves cleverly with those who can best serve their needs—as when, some years later, the Celts of Galatia side with Antiochus III of Syria against the Pergamese, whose territory they rule until 165 B.C. It is not the Greeks who finally defeat the Celts of Asia Minor but the Romans, who were rapidly expanding their empire into the Greek world. The Galatians finally submit and accept Roman citizenship but their national identity is strong enough for them to retain their name (as when St. Paul wrote his epistle to the Galatians in the middle of the first century A.D.) The distinctive Celtic language also survives until the fifth century A.D., as St. Jerome (translator of the Bible from Hebrew to Latin, and probably the world's greatest linguist) tells us that they spoke a language that was similar to that of the Gauls.

In Spain, the Celtiberians gradually lose out to Roman colonization. In 153 B.C. the Roman army besieges the Spanish Celtic hill fort of Numantia. The Celts negotiate a surrender, which is turned down by the Roman Senate. When they finally capitulate, they are massacred and the survivors sold into slavery. Over the next few years many attempts at rebellion are made, but few are successful. (Although one minor rebellion is successful when the Celts route the Roman army at the siege of the hill fort of Pallantia.) The second Roman siege of Numantia in Spain is orchestrated by slow starvation and the eventual massacre of all inhabitants and their leader, Avarus (133 B.C.).

The next great incursion into Celtic territory was the Romanization of Gaul. Southern Gaul is the first to be annexed and it includes the first major tribes to be defeated, the Arverni and the Allobroges. The Gauls had built massive hill fort defenses, which still dominate the landscape of southern France. These hill forts were called "oppidia" by the Romans. They were constructed of massive timber frames and rock insertions.

The first Roman governor to succeed in conquering the

Gauls was Julius Caesar, who went on to invade Britain. The final siege of Allesia (52 B.C.) ended Gallic resistance to Roman rule.

A.D. 41–55   The emperor Claudius orders the second invasion of Britain. The Romans' success is swift and decisive after the capture of Caratacos.

CARATACUS

One of the many Celtic heroes who attempted to defy the might of Rome, Caratacus was the son of Cunobelinos, which means "Hound of Belinos." Cunobelinos was the British king who had held out against the Romans for nine years. Caratacus had been betrayed by Cartimandua, Queen of the Brigantes, and taken to Rome along with his family and followers to be humiliated and publicly executed in a spectacle of Imperial triumph. Several accounts of his capture come down to us, such as that of Tacitus and Dio Cassius. The Romans, by all accounts, greatly respected him for his bravery and nobility of bearing. Dio Cassius tells us that when being dragged through the streets of Rome, Caratacus noted the splendor of the temples and civic buildings and remarked with sarcasm: "And why, when you have all this, do you still covet our miserable hovels in Britain?" Upon reaching the Capitoline Hill, he demanded to address the emperor Claudius and the Senate. He told them he was descended from a long line of illustrious princes that had control over extensive lands, and that he should have been treated as a worthy ally in his own right, equal to them. To find himself in such humiliating circumstances should not be a cause of triumph for them. Explaining himself, he said:

> I had arms, men, and horses; I had wealth in abundance; can you wonder that I am unwilling to lose them? The ambition of Rome aspires to universal domination; and must the rest of mankind, by consequence, stretch their necks to the yoke? I held you at

bay for years; had I acted otherwise, where, on your part, had been the glory of conquest, and where, on mine, the honour of a brave resistance? I am now in your power. If you are bent on vengeance, execute your purpose. The bloody scene will soon be over and the name of Caratacus will sink into oblivion. But if you preserve my life, then I shall be, to late posterity, a monument of Roman clemency.

His bold speech moved and impressed his audience and he and his family were granted clemency. However, they were forced to remain in exile in Rome, as permanent prisoners. Such was the personality of Caratacus that the Romans could not in all decency execute him. The year was A.D. 51, and the mighty empire was about to embark on the Romanization of Britain. Sparing Caratacus's life helped to secure the goodwill and cooperation of future client-kings.

A.D. 60   Less than a decade later, another famous British ruler, Queen Boudicca of the Iceni, organizes a rebellion against the Romans. The classical writers noted the fact that women in Celtic society held equality of rights with men, such as inheritance, the right to own property, and even to lead their followers in times of war. When Claudius invaded Britain, most of the tribes of the south capitulated and sought terms that allowed their rulers to become client-kings of the Empire and to maintain a certain amount of autonomy. The Iceni were the dominant group in what is now Essex and as far north as East Anglia. Their leader was called Prasutagus and his wife was Boudicca, whose name means "victory." After the death of Prasutagus, however, the Romans decide to discontinue the client-kingship, ignoring the position of Boudicca, who had inherited her husband's authority. They merely appropriate the tribal lands and set about colonizing them, establishing a colonial settlement at the old Iceni capital of Camulodunum (Colchester). This arouses resentment and protest as it becomes obvious that the Romans could break every agreement during a time of succession. Thus, the rebellion of Boudicca is one of the bloodiest in history, during which the Roman colonies of Camulodunum, Verulamium, and Londinium are destroyed and their inhabitants slaughtered. Particularly brutal is the impaling of the Roman women, on Boudicca's orders. Boudicca had called upon the Celtic gods, particularly the goddess Andrasta, for assistance. The rebellion took place at a time when the Romans were busily destroying the Celtic temples of the Druids in Anglesey. Upon their return, the Boudicca rebellion is savagely suppressed, and Tacitus tells us that about 80,000 Britons died. Boudicca commits suicide with her followers rather than accept defeat and humiliation; committing suicide after defeat was considered honorable. (The alternative was enslavement.) The famous sculpture of the Gaul killing his wife (now found in Rome) reminds us that this was a practice going back centuries. Cartimandua, Queen of the Brigantes, on the other hand, had usurped her husband's position after divorcing him and running off with his charioteer (her name means "sleek pony"). She was even prepared to breach the sacred law of hospitality by handing over Caratacus—with whom she had made a treaty—in chains to the Romans. After the rebellion of Boudicca, her estranged husband incited a rebellion against Cartimandua, and she eventually had to be rescued by the Romans.

A.D. 78   The Roman governor Agricola arrives in Britain. His account of events relating to the campaigns against the Caledonians as far north as the Firth of Moray, near Inverness in Scotland, were dictated to his son-in-law, Tacitus. Agricola reported on the speech made by the chieftain Calgacus of the Caledonians, before the Battle of Mons Graupius, in which he roused his followers to make a final stand against the Romans:

> We, the most distant dwellers upon earth, the last of the free . . . lie open to our enemies, and what men

know nothing about they always assume to be a valuable prize. But there are no more nations beyond us; nothing but waves and rocks, and the Romans, more deadly still than these—for in them is an arrogance which no submission or good behaviour can escape. Pillagers of the world, they have exhausted the land by their indiscriminate plunder. . . . To robbery, butchery and rapine they give the lying name of "government"; they create a desolation and call it peace.

Agricola's respect for his Celtic enemies, as well as his sense of justice—he had originally wanted to be a philosopher—are immortalized in this speech, which others would not have bothered to record.

Agricola had studied the battle tactics of the Celts, and his writings reveal that he had consulted Caesar's commentaries on Celtic chariot and guerrilla warfare. Routed, the rebels of the last unconquered corner of Celtic Britain lay open to the Romans, but the Caledonians (the Scottish tribes) did not submit. Later emperors and governors tried in vain to tame them. Hadrian built his wall considerably farther south, in A.D. 122, and Caracalla died in the attempt to contain them, in A.D. 211. The Antonine Wall, built in A.D. 142, between the Clyde and the Forth, was abandoned twenty years later.

Agricola claimed that Ireland could be taken with one legion. He kept in his court an Irish chieftan who has been exiled and who had promised to help the Romans invade Ireland; however, this invasion never materialized. His difficulty with rebellions in Celtic Britain may have deterred them, and it was difficult to conquer another country without an infra-structure: no cities, towns, or centralized authority. Over the next few centuries, the Picts (descendants of the Caledonians, nicknamed so because of their blue pigment skin decoration or tattoos) and the Irish constantly raided and harried the peripheries of Roman Britain. Then came the Saxon raids, and the eventual withdrawal of the Romans in A.D. 410. One such attack around A.D. 400 led by Niall of the Nine Hostages, king of Tara in Meath, leads to the capture of a young boy named Patrick. Christianity had been introduced into Roman Britain during the third century, along with another new religion, Mithraism, which was popular with the troops. In A.D. 432, Patrick brings Christianity to Ireland, and along with it a new and historical phase. The stimulus of Christianity led to an astonishing flowering of the arts in the service of the Church and the final expression of the La Tène art style, in manuscript, metalwork, and stone.

The Characters

AMAIRGIN: The first poet of Ireland, thought to possess power over nature

ANEIRIN: Welsh bard of the seventh century, author of *The Gododdin*

AIFÈ: Scottish queen, rival of Scathach in *The Táin*

BRAN: Hero of eighth century adventure tale who embarks on a journey to the Otherworld. When he returns to Ireland, he recounts his story and turns to dust

BRANWEN: Welsh love goddess, name means "White Raven." Principal character in *The Mabinogion*

CERRIDWYN: Goddess of knowledge and wisdom

CONCHOBAR: High King of Ulster in Ireland and head of the Ulster Branch Heroes, uncle of Cuchulainn

CUCHULAINN: The embodiment of strength and bravery, and hero of the Irish epic *The Táin*. Also known as the "Hound of Culain"

DAGDA: The "good god" and "good hand," earth god of life, prosperity, and knowledge

DANA: The mother goddess, ancestor of the Tuatha Dé Danann

DEIRDRE: Ill-fated heroine of the Irish saga *The Sons of Usnach*. From birth, she is a harbinger of misfortune to all who come in contact with her

EMER: The jealous wife of Cuchulainn, he who has many lovers and companions besides his spouse

EOCHAID AIREM: High King of Tara, lover of Étain

ERC: King of Leinster

EREC: Hero of Arthurian romance and husband of Enid. Together they were ideal lovers and partners. Erec is known as Gereint in *The Mabinogion*

ESA: The daughter of Eochaid Airem and Étain

ÉTAIN: Heroine and goddess of beauty and grace

FAND: Shape-shifting fairy queen of Ireland

FERDIAD: Friend and soul mate of Cuchulainn, persuaded by the devious Queen Medb to fight his friend

FINN MAC CUMHAIL: Hunter/warrior/poet of *The Fenian Cycle,* and the epitome of generosity and bravery

GALAHAD: Morally pure hero of Arthurian romance

GAWAIN: Hero of Arthurian romance and cousin of King Arthur

GUINEVERE: Wife of King Arthur who committed adultery with Lancelot and brought down a kingdom

GWALCHMEI: God of love and music, Welsh counterpart of Gawain, and nephew of Arthur

KEI: A principal player in King Arthur's court

KING ARTHUR: British hero-king of European literature from the twelfth to fifteenth centuries. Etymology of his name in Welsh is *Art* (bear) and *(g)wr* (hero). Main hero of *The Mabinogion,* the works of Chrétien de Troyes, and the *Lais* of Marie de France. First brought to fame by Geoffrey of Monmouth in the twelfth century

LANCELOT: Father of Galahad and paramour of Queen Guinevere

LLEVELYS: Brother of Lludd who becomes king of France and delivers his brother's kingdom from three plagues

LLUDD: Son of Beli Mawr, lead character in *The Mabinogion*

MABON: God of love and magic, taken as a small child from his mother in *The Mabinogion* and rescued with the help of King Arthur and animal wisdom

MACHA: Irish queen and goddess of war, fertility, and ritual games

MATH: Son of Mathonwy, principal character of *The Mabinogion.* Also Welsh god of love and enchantment

MEDB: The "Intoxicating One," warrior queen of Connacht and goddess of sex and fertility. Principal rival of Cuchulainn in *The Táin*

MIDIR: God of the Underworld; lover of Étain, sometimes depicted as the father and brother of the Dagda

MORRIGAN: Irish goddess of death and war who often appears as a raven

PRYDERI: Shape-shifting god and son of Rhiannon and Pwyll in *The Mabinogion*

RHIANNON: Principal character of *The Mabinogion,* renowned for her quick tongue

SCATHACH: The war goddess who trained Cuchulainn and many other heroes in arms; her name means "in shadow" and "in protection of." Taught Cuchulainn his famous aggressive leap

TALIESIN: Late sixth century Welsh poet, thought to possess other-worldly powers

The Works

The Annals of Ulster: Twelfth century record of the major historical events in Ireland

The Book of Aneirin: Welsh manuscript that includes the poem *Y [The] Gododdin*

The Book of the Dean of Lismore: A collection of Scottish herioc ballads translated by James MacGregor in the early sixteenth century

The Book of Invasions: Twelfth century Irish work containing myths, legends, and genealogies

The Book of Taliesin: Thirteenth century Welsh manuscript containing sixty poems by Taliesin

The Dindshenchas: Collection of local legends that details the names of rivers, forts, lakes, and heroic figures of Ireland

The Brehon Laws: The ancient laws of Ireland, dating from around A.D. 438

The Bruce: Epic fourteenth century Scottish poem by John Barbour celebrating the life and valor of Robert the Bruce, the Scottish hero who fought the British for an indepedent nation

The Mabinogion: The masterpiece of Welsh literature; includes the four books of The Mabinogi (Pwyll, Branwen, Manawydan, and Math), as well as twelve other tales

The Scottish Miracle Plays: From Cornwall, Christian fables that celebrate the "The Legend of the Rood" and "The Oil of Mercy"

Táin Bó Cuailnge: The greatest work of Irish classical literature, first written down in the seventh and eighth centuries

The Ulster Cycle: Irish prose and verse romances featuring the traditional heroes of Ulster

Animals

"When clouds of locusts invade their country and damage the crops, the Celts invoke certain prayers and offer sacrifices which charm birds—and the birds hear these prayers, come in flocks, and destroy the locusts. If however, one of them should capture one of these birds, his punishment according the laws of the country is death. If he is pardoned and released, this throws the birds into a rage, and to revenge the captured bird they do not respond if they are called on again."

—Aelian, on the sacredness of
animals in the Celtic world

Throughout Celtic literature, there is an almost divine reverence for the animal world. From the La Tène period to the Middle Ages, birds, horses, oxen, boars, and fish hold an especially powerful place in Celtic mythology. In Irish, Scottish, and Welsh storytelling, ancient gods and heroes transform themselves into animals, and often seek their help in rescuing fellow warriors. For example, in *The Mabinogion*, Arthur's knights ask the Salmon of Llyn Llyw for help in rescuing Mabon, son of Modron, from a prisoner's enclosure. In the Scottish poems from *The Dean of Lismore*, Caoilte Mac Ronan uses animals to save Finn from Cormac McArt, King of Ireland. In *The Táin*, the bull figures prominently, and represents wealth, strength, and virility. According to James McKillop's *The Dictionary of Celtic Mythology*, Finnbenach (the white bull) and Donn Cuailnge (the brown bull) are the most celebrated in Celtic literature and are believed to have possessed divine powers. In Celtic ritual, Druids, the religious leaders of ancient Ireland, participated in a "bull sleep," a rite in which men killed the bull, ate his flesh, and drank his blood in order to achieve clairvoyant powers.

In the mythology of all the Celtic countries, animals are portrayed as majestic messengers of God. Even when they are killed, their death is seen as imparting a higher spiritual knowledge to the men who consume them.

From *The Two Bulls:*

The story of The Two Bulls *from* Táin Bó Cuailnge *is one of the most renowned in ancient Irish literature, and best embodies the Celtic belief that animals have extraordinary magical powers. Like the horse, the bull is pervasive in Celtic mythology. It is in this selection that we are introduced to the most famous—the White-horned and the Brown bull, mythical beasts thought to have originally been fairy swineherds. It is also fascinating—and typical—in this story that Medb, queen of Connacht, is willing to wage war over these beasts, and that she takes advice from a shape-changing eel without question.*

One day Medb went out to the spring, with a small bronze vessel in her hand, and she dipped it in the water, and the little eel went into it, and every colour was to be seen on him. And she was a long time looking at him, she thought the colours were so beautiful. Then the water went away, and the eel was alone in the vessel. "It is a pity you cannot speak to me," said Medb. "What is it you want to know?" said the eel. "I would like to know what way it is with you in the shape of a beast," she said; "and I would like to know what will happen to me after I get the sway over Connacht." "Indeed it is a tormented beast I am," he said, "and it is in many shapes I have been. And as to yourself," he said, "handsome as you are, you should take a good man to be with you in your sway." "I have no wish," said Medb, "to let a man of Connacht get the upper hand over me." And with that she went home again. But she married Ailill after that, and as for the eel, he was swallowed down by one of Medb's cows that came to drink at the spring.

And it was from that cow, and from the cow that belonged to Daire, son of Fachna, the two bulls were born, the White-horned and the Brown. They were the finest ever seen in Ireland, and gold and silver were put on their horns by the men of Connacht. In Connacht, no bull dared bellow before the White-horned, and in Ulster, no boar dare bellow before the Brown.

As to the Brown, he that had been Friuch, the Munster swineherd, his lowing when he would be coming home every evening to his yard was good music to the people of the whole of Cuailnge. And wherever he was, neither Bocanachs nor Bananachs nor witches of the valley, could come into the one place with him. And it was on account of him the great war broke out.

Now, when Medb saw at Ilgaireth that the battle was going against her, she sent eight of her own messengers to bring away the Brown Bull, and his heifers. "For whoever goes back or does not go back," she said, "the Brown Bull must go to Cruachan."

Now, when the Brown Bull came into Connacht, and saw the beautiful trackless country before him, he let three great loud bellowings out of him. As soon as the White-horned heard that, he set out for the place those bellowings came from, with his head high in the air. Then Medb said that the men of her army must not go to their homes till they would see the fight between the two bulls. And they all said someone must be put to watch the fight, and to give a fair report of it afterwards. And it is what they agreed, that Bricriu should be sent to watch it, because he had not taken any side in the war; for he had been through the whole length of it under care of physicians at Cruachan, with the dint of the wound he got the day he vexed Fergus, and that Fergus drove the chess-men into his head. "I will go willingly," said Bricriu. So he went out and took his place in a gap, where he could have a good view of the fight.

As soon as the bulls caught sight of one another they pawed the earth so furiously that they sent the sods flying, and their eyes were like balls of fire in their heads; they locked their horns together, and they ploughed up the ground under them and trampled it, and they were trying to crush and to destroy one another through the whole length of the day.

And once the White-horned went back a little way and made a rush at the Brown, and got his horn in his side, and he gave out a great bellow, and they rushed both together through the gap where Bricriu was, the way he was trodden into the earth under their feet. And that is how Bricriu of the Bitter Tongue, son of Cairbre, got his death.

—IRELAND, 8TH CENTURY

From *The Senchus Mor:*

In this selection from the Brehon Laws, we see that animals were given their own rights.

The cat is exempt from liability for injuring an idler in catching mice when mousing; and half fine is due from for the profitable worker whom he may injure, and the excitement of his mousing takes the other half off him.

—IRELAND, C. A.D. 438

From *The Dean Of Lismore:*

In this selection, Caoilte Mac Ronan enlists the help of animals to save his friend Finn from the hands of Cormac McArt, King of Ireland.

From Taura I a journey took,
A journey over all the land.

I gathered in the flocks of birds,
Though they were so very scattered.
Two fierce geilts I brought along,
And two fine tall and clawed ospreys,
And ravens from Fee ya von:
Two wild ducks from Loch a Sellin,
Two crows down from Slieve Cullin
Two wild oxen brought from Borrin
Two swans I brought from Dobhran gorm . . .
A bull and cow in calf from Drumcan,
These I had from Muirn Munchain.
Ten hounds of the hounds of the Feinn
Did Cormac insolently require.
Whatever thing he asked of me,
I brought it with me as I came.
When I had them all collected,
And brought them to one plain,
And sought to have them in control,
They all of them did scatter widely.
The raven flew away to the south,
A cause of me to much vexation;
I caught it in Glen da bhan,
By the side of deep Loch Lurgan.
The duck did also me forsake,
Nor was it easier to take it;
Over swift and swollen streams,
I chased it to Achin Dughlas.
Then I seized it by the neck,
Although it was not very willing.
I took this duck along with me
That I might liberate Finn from Cormac.

—SCOTLAND, C. 16TH CENTURY

From *The Mabinogion:*

In this magical scene from The Mabinogion, *animals are once again called upon to rescue their human counterparts. Here, King Arthur entrusts the birds and animals to help him free Mabon, one of the men of his court, from prison, and indeed he is rewarded in his faith, when the Salmon of Llyn Llyw carries Kei and Gwrhyr, two of Arthur's men to the prison where Mabon is being held.*

So Arthur and the warriors of Britain rose and went forth to seek Eiddoel, and they came to the outer wall of Glini's fortress, where Eiddoel was held prisoner. Glini stood on top of the wall and said, "Arthur, since you will not leave me in peace on this rock, what do you want of me? I have no good and no pleasure here, neither wheat nor oats, and now you come to do me harm." "I have not come to do you harm," Arthur replied, "only to ask for the prisoner you hold." "I did not intend to give him to anyone, but I will give him to you, and you shall have my support and strength as well." Then the men said to Arthur, "Lord, go back, for you ought not to accompany the host on this sort of petty errand." "Gwrhyr Interpreter of Languages," said Arthur, "it will be proper for you to go on this errand, for you know all tongues and can speak with some of the birds and animals. Eiddoel, it is right for you to accompany my men in seeking your cousin. Kei and Bedwyr, I hope that you will obtain whatever you seek—go on this errand on my behalf."

These men went on until they found the Ousel of Kilgwri, and Gwrhyr asked, "For God's sake, do you know anything of Mabon son of Modron, who when three nights old was stolen away from between his mother and the wall?" "When I first came here," answered the ousel, "there was a smith's anvil. I was a young bird then, and since that time no work has been done on the anvil except by my beak every night. Today there is not so much as a nut that has not been worn away, and yet God's revenge on me if in all that time I have heard anything of the man you seek. Nevertheless, I will do what is right by Arthur's messengers. There is a kind of creature which God made even before me, and I will guide you to it."

They then went to the Stag of Rhedenvre and said, "Stag of Rhedenvre, we are Arthur's messengers, and we have come to you because we know of no animal which is older. Tell us if you know anything of Mabon son of Modron, who was stolen from his mother when three nights old." "When I first came here," said the stag, "there was only a single antler on either side of my head, and no tree here but a single hazel oak which then grew into an oak of one hundred branches; thereafter the tree fell and today there is nothing left but a red stump. I have been here since that day and have heard nothing of the man you seek, but since you are Arthur's messengers, I will guide you to an animal which God made before me."

They came to the Owl of Cwm Cawlwyd and said, "Owl of Cwm Cawlwyd, these are messengers from Arthur. Do you know anything of Mabon son of Modron, who was stolen from his mother when three nights old?" "If I knew I would tell you. When I first came here the great valley which you see before you was a wooded glen; the race of man came and destroyed it, whereupon a second forest grew up, and this forest is the third. As for me, my wings are now nothing but stumps. To this day I have heard nothing of the man you seek, but I will guide Arthur's messengers to the oldest animal in the world and the one which has travelled the most, the Eagle of Gwernabwy."

Gwrhyr then said, "Eagle of Gwernabwy, we are messengers from Arthur who have come to ask if you know anything of Mabon son of Modron, who was stolen from his mother when three nights old." "I came here long ago," answered the eagle, "and when I first came I had a stone from the top of which I pecked at the stars every evening, and now that stone is not a hand's-breadth in height. I have been here from that day to this, and I have heard nothing of the man you seek except when I made a trip to look for food at Llyn Llyw. There I sank my claws into a salmon, expecting that it would feed me for a long time, but it drew me down into the water, so that I barely escaped. I returned with all my relatives to destroy the fish, but it sent messengers to make peace, and came itself to have fifty tridents pulled out of its back. Unless this salmon knows something of the one you seek, I know of none who might know anything. I will guide you to it."

They came to that place, and the eagle said, "Salmon of Llyn Llyw, I have come with Arthur's messengers to ask if you know anything of Mabon son of Modron, who was stolen from his mother when three nights old." "I will tell you as much as I know. I swim upstream on every tide until I reach Gloucester, where I found such evil as I had never found before. That you may believe me, let one of you ride on my shoulders." So Kei and Gwrhyr rode on the salmon's shoulders until they came to the prisoner's enclosure, and they heard moaning and wailing from the other side of the wall, and Gwrhyr said, "Who is crying in this stone house?" "Alas, there is reason for this man to lament: Mabon son of Modron is here, and no one was ever so harshly imprisoned, not Lludd Silver Hand, not Greid son of Eri." "Is there any hope of securing your release through gold or silver or worldly wealth, or through battle and fighting?" "Such release as is got for me will be got by fighting." So they returned to Arthur and told him where Mabon's prison was; Arthur summoned the warriors of this island and went to Gloucester where Mabon was prisoner, but Kei and Bedwyr rode on the salmon's shoulders. While Arthur's men were fighting at the fortress, Kei broke through the wall of the enclosure and rescued the prisoner on his back, besides fighting with the men; then Arthur returned home, and with him Mabon, a free man.

—WALES, 14TH CENTURY

From *The Dean Of Lismore:*

The horse is one of the most revered and celebrated animals in Celtic literature. In this poem from The Dean of Lismore, *Finlay the red-haired Bard pays tribute to the majesty and beauty of the beast.*

Gael-like is every leap of the dun horse,
A Gael is she in truth.
It is she who conquers and wins,
In all that I'll now sing.
The praise of speed to her limbs,
In every fierce assault.
Marked, and famous her strength,
While quiet at the house of prayer.
The birds are who they could,
Strive with her in the race.
Not false is the fame of that horse,
The steed both sturdy and swift,
Liker she was to Duseivlin,
Than to the beast of Lamacha,
They who would view her size and triumphs,
Can nowhere find her match.
Just like the wheeling of the mountain winds,
Is the action of the prancing steed.
Hundreds admire her paces,
Like one in frenzy passing.
Like the point of an arrow this horse,
Famous are all her doings.
Bands of the great witness her course,
As with speed she rushes.
Though far before her stands the groom,
No blunderer is her rider.
Few are the words would tell her praise,

Like birds on wing are her movements.
Her triumphs and paces the same,
Whether 'mong rocks or bogs she moves.
Before that horse all men so fear,
When she comes in the trappings of war.
In the troop, the hunt, or the conflict,
That horse a noble horse is.
That horse is all full of spirit,
As fameworthy she follows the banner.
That wave-like steed, hardy and keen,
Will win for her rider the praise of men.
Forth from her stall she takes the lead,
That gentle, great, and active horse.
She will triumph in speed and slaughter,
Til that day in evening sinks.
Ready to treasure the girdle of gold,
The field with violence shakes.
Startling, rounded, bright, well shod,
Gentle, broad-backed, coloured well.
A horse of such great fame as this,
I long had heard that they possessed.
Where was ever found her match,
Not he, the beast of Lamacha.
MacGregor's the master of that horse,
Prince of the house to poet's free.
From Banva men do come to praise,
To Albion they do come to seek,
The man who robs from the Saxon,
And e'er puts his trust in the Gael.

—SCOTLAND, C. 16TH CENTURY

Arthur

"Arthur began to increase his personal entourage by inviting very distinguished men from far-distant kingdoms to join it. In this way, he developed such a code of courtliness in his household that he inspired peoples living far away to imitate him. The result was that even the man of noblest birth, once he was roused to rivalry, thought nothing at all of himself unless he wore his arms and dressed in the same way as Arthur's knights. At last the fame of Arthur's generosity and bravery spread to the very ends of the earth; and the kings of countries far across the sea trembled at the thought that they might be attacked and invaded by him."
— Geoffrey of Monmouth, on the glorious
legend of King Arthur

The legend of King Arthur remains one of the most pervasive—and controversial—in Celtic literature. In the twelfth century, the Welsh monk, Geoffrey of Monmouth, first brought widespread renown to Arthur in his book, *History of the Kings of Britain,* which was to become the definitive book of the Middle Ages. In his history, Geoffrey details Arthur's life from his birth as the son of Uther Pendragon, his marriage to Ganhumara, a lady of Roman lineage, and his reign as king of the Britons, during which he led the sixth-century Britons, who were the ancestors to all the Celts, to victory over the Saxons and Angles. *The Annals of Ulster,* the chronicle history of Ireland, also contains an entry that marks the death of Arthur's father, Uther Pendragon, in A.D. 467. This entry was originally found in St. Cuana's seventh century chronicle, *The Book of Cuana*, and suggests that Arthur's life was more than just a work of fiction.

To this day, scholars continue to debate Arthur's existence as an actual historical figure. In his history, *The Decline and Fall of the Roman Empire*, historian Edward Gibbon maintains that Arthur did exist, while Geoffrey Ashe in his book *The Quest for Arthur's Britain* argues that no real proof of Arthur's life has ever been found. It is also widely debated whether the presence of the wizard Merlin began in the British, Celtic, or French texts.

While there are many scholars who believe that Arthur's reign remains a figment of the imaginations of overzealous and overly creative medieval ecclesiastics, his influence cannot be denied. From the great Welsh work, *The Mabinogion*, to the French Arthurian tales of Chrétien de Troyes and medieval Irish legend, Arthur remains the epitome of the Celtic ideal—heroic, loyal, strong, and pure in motive.

Arthur's legend continues to inspire modern literature, and its influence can be found today in the works of J.R.R. Tolkien, C.S. Lewis, and even more recently in those of J.K. Rowling. It is also fascinating to note that some form of the Arthur story can be found in almost every culture from Dutch to French to Italian. All of these versions are remarkable in their similarity, which implies that the legend of Arthur is much more than a mere myth.

From *Erec et Enide:*

Chrétien de Troyes (c. 1140–1200) was the first chronicler of the King Arthur tales. In this selection from Erec et Enide, *a story that also appears as* Gereint and Enid *in the Welsh* Mabinogion, *he depicts the glory, sense of honor, and sheer splendor that surrounded Arthur's Court.*

One Easter Day in the springtime, King Arthur held court in his town of Cardigan. Never was there seen so rich a court; for

many a good knight was there, hardy, bold, and brave, and rich
ladies and damsels, gentle and fair daughters of kings. But before
the court was disbanded, the king told his knights that he wished
to hunt the White Stag, in order to observe worthily the ancient
custom. When my lord Gawain heard this, he was sore displeased
and said: "Sire, you will derive neither thanks nor goodwill from
this hunt. We all know long since what this custom of the White
Stag is: whoever can kill the White Stag must forsooth kiss the
fairest maiden of your court, come what may. But of this there
might come great ill: for there are five hundred damsels of high
birth, gentle and prudent daughters of kings, and there is none of
them but has a bold and valiant knight for her lover who would be
ready to contend, whether right or wrong, that she who is his lady
is the fairest and gentlest of them all." The king replies: "That I
know well; yet I will not desist on that account; for a king's word
ought never to be gainsaid. To-morrow morning we shall all gaily
go to hunt the White Stag in the forest of adventure. And very
delightful this hunt will be."

And so the affair is arranged for the next morning at daybreak. The morrow, as soon as it is day, the king gets up and
dresses, and dons a short jacket for his forest ride. He commands
the knights to be aroused and the horses to be made ready.
Already they are ahorse, and off they go, with bows and arrows.
After them the queen mounts her horse, taking a damsel with her.
A maid she was, the daughter of a king, and she rode a white palfrey. After them there swiftly followed a knight named Erec, who
belonged to the Round Table, and had great fame at the court. Of
all the knights that ever there were, never one received such
praise: and he was so fair that nowhere in the world need one seek
a fairer knight than he. He was very fair, brave, and courteous,
though not yet twenty-five years old. Never was there a man of his
age of greater knighthood. And what shall I say of his virtues?
Mounted on his horse, and clad in an ermine mantle, he came

galloping down the road, wearing a coat of splendid flower silk which was made at Constantinople. He had put on hose of brocade, well made and cut, and when his golden spurs were well attached, he sat securely in his stirrups. He carried no arm with him but his sword. As he galloped along, at the corner of a street he came up with the queen, and said: "My lady, if it please you, I should gladly accompany you along this road, having come for no other purpose than to bear you company." And the queen thanks him: "Fair friend, I like your company well, in truth; for better I could not have."

—FRANCE, C. A.D. 1170

From *The Mabinogion:*

In this scene from How Culhwch Won Olwen, *King Arthur shows his generosity and great love of family when he comes to the joyful realization that Culhwch is his cousin.*

"My heart grows tender towards you, and I know that you must come from my lineage. Tell me who you are." "I am Culhwch son of Kilydd son of the ruler Kelyddon, and Goleuddydd daughter of the ruler Amlawdd is my mother." Arthur said, "That is true. You are my first cousin—therefore state your desire and you shall have it, whatever mouth and tongue may name." "In God's truth, and the truth of your kingdom?" "You shall have it gladly." "Then I ask for Olwen daughter of Chief Giant Ysbaddaden, and I invoke her in the name of your warriors."

—WALES, 14TH CENTURY

From *the Annals Of Ulster, Vol. 1:*

In this entry, we are given a fascinating date–the death of Uther Pendragon, Arthur's father—and a compelling authentic factual record of Arthur's existence, which was first noted by St. Cuana in the seventh century.

Kal. Jan (Sund, m. 10) A.D. 467

Rest of Benignus the bishop, successor of Patrick. The feast of Tara held by Ailill Molt (son of Dathi, son of Fiachra, son of Eochaid Muidhemhoin). So I find in the book of Cuana. Death of Uter Pendragon, King of England, to whom succeeded his son, i.e. King Arthur, i.e. who ordained the Round Table.

—IRELAND, C. A.D. 1200

From the poem *A Vision:*

In this poem, the great Irish Bardic poet Tadhg Dall Ohuiginn (1550–1591) describes a mythical and luminous woman who is so splendid that she can only be a part of King Arthur's court.

Art thou the woman who was here last night with me in a vision? Uncertain about thee as I am, thou bright form, my mind is bewildered.

If thou she not be who came before, O slender figure, gentle and soft of hand, and dainty of step, thou art exactly similar.

Thy glowing cheek, thy blue eye—never were formed from the four-fold element two more similar in form, O yellow, curly plaited locks.

Thy white teeth, thy crimson lips which make sufficing lullaby, brown brows of the hue of the sloe, and all that lies between them.

Throat like the blossom of the lily, long slender hands; supple, plump flesh, of the hue of the waves, dulling the whiteness of the river's foam.

Small, smooth, white breasts rising above a lovely, shining slope; gentle expanses, with borders most fair and delightful, they are to be likened to fairy knolls.

On the ends of thy luxuriant tresses are flocks not usual in winter, which have been bathed in gold, a most wondrous flock.

I am worthy of trust, thou art in no danger, tell me was it

thou who came before to the land of Fal, to trouble me, thou shining white-toothed, modest-faced lady?

Or art she who came afore-time to visit the Round Table,
thou head of smooth, fair, bright locks, to wondrous King Arthur?

—IRELAND, C. A.D. 1570

From *The Mabinogion:*

*In this passage, King Arthur shows his unwavering courage by
declaring his decision to fight his fiercest enemy, even without the
aide of his men, from* How Culhwch Won Olwen.

"Twrch Trwyth has killed a number of my men. By the
courage of man, he shall not go into Cornwall while I am alive,
nor will I pursue him further, rather I will pit my life against his.
You men may do as you wish."

—WALES, 14TH CENTURY

The Mabinogion:

*The warrior Iddawg swears his devotion to his leader to fellow
warrior Rhonabwy, from* The Dream of Rhonabwy.

"The Emperor Arthur has never fled, and had that remark
been overheard, you would now be a dead man."

—WALES, 14TH CENTURY

From *The Lais:*

In this seminal poem from her book of lais *entitled* Lanval,
*Marie de France, often renowned as the greatest woman writer of
medieval literature, depicts Arthur as the generous hero king—
with a twist. Arthur rewards all of the men of his court for their
bravery, but he neglects the hero of the story, Lanval, even though
he possesses all of the traits so cherished by the court of the Round
Table. It is most interesting to note that this is the only Arthur*

story written by a woman, and it is the only version that gives a
less romanticized view of Arthur and the men of his court. Little
is known of Marie de France's life, but we do know that she was
supremely educated, connected to the English court, and dedicated
her book of Lais *to Henry II.*

The adventure of another lay,
Just as it happened, I'll relay:
It tells of a very nice nobleman,
And it's called Lanval in Breton.
King Arthur was staying at Carduel—
That King of valiant and courtly estate—
His borders there he guarded well
Against the Pict, against the Scot,
Who'd cross into Logres to devastate
The countryside often, and a lot.
He held court there at Pentecost,
The summer feast we call Whitsun,
Giving gifts of impressive cost
To every count and each baron
And all knights of the Round Table.
Never elsewhere so many, such able
Knights assembled! Women and land
He shared with all—except one vassal
Who'd served him well; he forgot Lanval.
Lanval got nothing at the King's hand.
For being brave and generous,
For his beauty and his prowess,
He was envied by all the court;
Those who claimed to hold him dear,
If Fortune had brought him up short,
Would not have shed a kindly tear.
A king's son, he'd a noble lineage,

But now, far from his heritage,
He'd joined the household of the King.
He'd spent all the money he could bring
Already. The King gave him no more—
He gave just what Lanval asked for.
Now Lanval knows not what to do;
He's very thoughtful, very sad.
My lords, I don't astonish you:
A man alone, with no counsel—or bad—
A stranger in a strange land
Is sad, when no help's at hand.

—FRANCE, C. A.D. 1170

Battle

"Their aspect is terrifying. . . . They are very tall in stature with rippling muscles under clear white skin. Their hair is blond, but not naturally so: they bleach it, to this day artificially, washing it in lime and combing it back from their foreheads. They look like wood-demons, their hair is thick and shaggy like a horse's mane . . ."

—Diodorus Siculus, on first witnessing the fearsome Celts preparing to do battle

There were perhaps none more skilled and fearless in battle than the Celtic warriors. From childhood, Celtic warriors learned the skills necessary to defeat their opponents, no matter how formidable. The classical writer Strabo was so stirred by the Celts' seeming fearlessness that he called them "madly fond of war, high spirited and quick to battle" and claimed that, "When they are stirred up they assemble in their bands for battle, quite openly and without forethought." Similarly, Polybius recounted their absolute ferocity against the Romans on the battlefield in his histories: "Though almost cut to pieces, they held their ground with unabated courage." Livy observed after watching them in battle, "When the Celtiberians saw that the battle-lines arrayed in pitched battle and they were not a match for the legions, they made a thrust with the wedge, in which manner of fighting they are so powerful that against whatever troops they drive their charge, they cannot be charged."

In Celtic literature, the importance of skill in battle pervades all of the major works. For example, in *The Mabinogion*, we see that this intrepidity as well as knowledge and cunning prove to be just as important as strength in battle. Llevelys's sage advice to his brother Lludd is crucial in saving the kingdom from the enemy, the Corranyeid. The Irish chronicle *The Annals of Ulster* marks the deaths of heroes killed in battle and praises their skills and heroism on the battlefield. In the Irish epic *The Táin*, prowess in battle is the most coveted skill that the hero, Cuchulainn, can possess. There is perhaps no better example of the importance of battle in Celtic literature than that of the sixth century Welsh epic poem, *The Gododdin*, which celebrates the lives of those who died in the harrowing Battle of Catraeth. These Welsh warriors are the embodiment of strength and skill in battle, as well as true bravery in the face of defeat.

In the ancient Celtic era, warriors took to the battlefield with dignity, grace, and without hesitation. It can be said that the way in which a warrior fought and died in battle was as important as the way he lived.

From *The Senchus Mor*:

In this selection from the Brehon Laws, we see that battle was such an integral part of daily life in ancient Ireland that it required its own provision.

The exemption of a combatant from one day to another or to the end of a week. This is in the case of a battle from one day to another for a week, i.e. a battle between two territories, or two provinces, with due notice. The combatant is exempt from crime for killing his own antagonist in the battle from one day to another. The time is extended to the end of a week if the battle is between two provinces or between Galls and Gads. The exemption in case of injury by a flail in a kiln comes next. There is exemption for that which the flail breaks in the kiln. If a person comes under it, there is compensation for injury to fellow-labourers, if they are face to face; if side by side, the fine is one third of compensation. There is exemption for whatever injury the flail does to every sensible adult who has sight, and there is compensation due for injury due to animals and non-sensible persons, and to such as are asleep and to everyone who has not sight.

—IRELAND, C. A.D. 438

The epic sixth century Welsh poem, The Goddodin, *written by Aneirin, is a requiem for the Welsh warrior aristocracy, who would lose all but a few of their three hundred men in the battle at Catraeth. In these verses, the warriors of the Gododdin take to the battlefield willingly and nobly, although they face certain defeat at the hands of ten thousand Englishmen.*

Men went to Gododdin, laughing warriors,
Assailants in a savage war-band
They slaughtered with swords in short order,
War-column of kind-hearted Rhaithfyw.

Men went to Catraeth, keen their war-band.
Pale mead their portion, it was poison.
Three hundred under orders to fight.
And after celebration, silence.
Though they went to churches for shriving,
True is the tale, death confronted them.

Men went to Catraeth, mead-nourished band,
Great the disgrace should I not praise them.
With huge dark-socketed crimson spears,
Stern and steadfast the battle-hounds fought.

Of Brennych's band I'd hardly bear it
Should I leave a single man alive.
A comrade I lost, faithful I was,
Keen in combat, leaving him grieves me.
No desire had he for a dowry,
Y Cian's young son, of Maen Gwyngwn.

Men went to Catraeth at dawn:
All their fears had been put to flight.
Three hundred clashed with ten thousand.
They stained their spears ruddy with blood.
He held firm, bravest in battle,
Before Mynyddawg Mwynfawr's men.

Men went to Catraeth at dawn:
Their high spirits lessened their life-spans.
They drank mead, gold and sweet, ensnaring;
For a year the minstrels were merry.
Red their swords, let the blades remain
Uncleansed, white shields and four-sided spearheads,
Before Mynyddawg Mwynfawr's men.

Men went to Catraeth at morn.
He made certain the shame of armies;
They made sure that a bier was needed.
The most savage blades in Christendom,
He contrived, no request for a truce,
A blood-path and death for his foeman.
When he was before Gododdin's band
Neirthiad's deeds showed a hero's bold heart.

—WALES, c. 6TH CENTURY

The ancient Irish tale The Second Battle of Mag Tured *recounts the heroic rise of the Tuatha Dé Danann. In this selection, Dagda, the "good god" is preparing for battle with the Femorians and calls upon the wise men of Ireland to help him outwit and overpower the enemy.*

Thereafter the wizards of Ireland were summoned to them, and their medical men and charioteers and smiths and farmers and lawyers. They held speech with them in secret. Then Nuada inquired of the sorcerer whose name was Mathgen, what power he could wield? He answered that through his contrivance he would cast the mountains of Ireland on the Femorians, and roll their summits against the ground. And he declared to them that the twelve chief mountains of the land of Erin would support the Tuatha Dé Danann, in battling for them, to wit, Sliab League, and Denna Ulad and the Mourne Mountains, and Bri Ruri and Sliab Bladma and Sliab Snechtai, Sliab Mis and Blai-sliab and Nevin and Sliab Maccu Belgadan and Segais and Cruachan Aigle.

Then he asked the cupbearer what power he could wield. He answered that he would bring the twelve chief lochs of Ireland before the Femorians, and that they would not find water therein, whatever thirst might seize them. These are those lochs: Dergloch, Loch Luimnigh, Loch Corrib, Loch Ree, Loch Mask, Strangford Loch, Belfast Loch, Loch Neagh, Loch Foyle, Loch Gara, Loch Reag, Marloch. They would betake themselves to the twelve chief rivers of Ireland: Bush, Boyne, Baa, Nem, Lee, Shannon, Moy, Sligo, Erne, Finn, Liffey, Suir; and they will all be hidden from the Femorians, so that they will not find a drop therein. Drink shall be provided for the men of Ireland, though they bide in the battle to the end of seven years.

Then said Figol son of Mamos, their Druid: "I will cause

three showers of fire to pour on the faces of the Femorian host, and I will take out of them two thirds of their valour and their bravery and their strength, and I will bind their urine in their own bodies and in the bodies of their horses. Every breath that the men of Ireland shall exhale will be an increase in valor and bravery and strength to them. Though they bide in the battle till the end of seven years, they will not be weary in any wise."

Said the Dagda: "The power which ye boast I shall wield it all by myself." "It is thou art the Dagda (good hand), with everyone": wherefore thenceforward the name "Dagda" adhered to him. Then they separated from the council, agreeing to meet again that day three years.

Now when the provision of the battle had then been settled, Lugh and Dagda and Ogma went to the three gods of Danu, and these gave Lugh the plan of the battle; and for seven years they were preparing for it and making their weapons.

—IRELAND, 8TH CENTURY

In this selection from The Mabinogion, *the two brothers, Lludd and Llevelys, show that, in battle, their cunning more than their force helps to rid the country of the three plagues that threaten to bring ruin to their land.*

When Lludd told his brother the purpose of his errand, Llevelys said that he knew already why Lludd had come. Then they sought some different way to discuss the problem, so that the wind could not carry it off and the Corannyeid learn of their conversation. Llevelys ordered a long horn of bronze to be made, and they spoke through that, but whatever one said to the other came out as hateful and contrary. When Llevelys perceived there was a devil frustrating them and causing trouble, he ordered wine to be poured through the horn to wash it out, and the power of the wine drove the devil out. Thereafter they conversed unhindered. Llevelys told his brother that he would give him some insects, and that Lludd should keep some alive for breeding, in case the plague returned, but that he should take the remaining insects and mash them with water, for Llevelys assured his brother that this mixture would be effective in destroying the Corannyeid. When Lludd arrived home he was to summon all the people of his realm, both his own race and that of the Corannyeid, under pretence of making peace between them, and when all were assembled he was to take this purifying water and throw it over everyone, for Llevelys assured him that the water would poison the Corannyeid without killing or injuring his own people. "The second plague in your realm," said Llevelys, "is a dragon. A dragon of another race, a foreign one, is fighting with it and struggling to overcome it, and therefore your dragon screams horribly. This is how you can see for yourself: when you arrive home, measure the length and breadth of the island, and where you find the exact centre have a pit dug; in the pit place a vat full of the best mead that can be made, with a silk sheet over the vat, and guard this yourself. You will see the dragons fighting in the shape of monstrous animals until they finally rise into the air as dragons, and when they have wearied of their horrid and frightening combat, they will sink onto the sheet in the form of two little pigs; they will drag the sheet to the bottom of the vat, and there they will drink the mead and fall asleep. When that happens you must wrap the sheet round them and lock them in a stone chest, and bury them in the earth within the strongest place you know of in the island. As long as they are within that strong place no plague will come to Britain. As for the third plague, a mighty magician is carrying off your food and drink from the banquet table. His spells and enchantments cause everyone to fall asleep, so you will have to stand watch yourself lest sleep overcome you too, have a vat of cold water close by, and when you feel sleepy step into the vat."

Then Lludd returned to his own country, and at once he summoned both his own people and the Corannyeid. He mashed the insects with water as Llevelys had instructed, and threw this mixture over the entire assembly, and at once destroyed all of the Corannyeid without harming any of the British. A little later Lludd had the length and breadth of the island measured and found its centre to be in Oxford. There he had a pit dug, and in the pit he set a vat of the best mead that could be made, with a silk sheet over the vat, and he himself watched that night and saw the dragons fighting. When they were tired and worn out they sank onto the sheet and dragged it down to the bottom of the vat, where they drank up the mead and fell asleep. Lludd wrapped the sheet round them and locked them in a stone chest in the most secure place he could find in Eryri, and thereafter the place was called Dinas Emreis, though before it had been Dinas Ffaraon Dandde (Ffaraon Dandde was one of the Three Noble Youths who broke his heart with dismay). Thus ended the tempestuous screaming in the kingdom. Then Lludd ordered a great feast to be set out, and a vat of cold water to be prepared and set nearby, and he himself stood guard, armed with his weapons. About the third watch of the night he heard many songs and much excellent entertainment, until the drowsiness of sleep stole over him; lest this sleep overcome him and frustrate his intent, he immersed himself in the water repeatedly. Finally a huge man clad in strong heavy armour entered with a basket, and as was his custom he put all the food and drink that had been prepared and set out into the basket and made off. Lludd thought nothing so strange as that the basket could hold so much. He set off after the giant, crying, "Stop! Stop! Though you have done many wrongs and inflicted many losses you shall do so no more, unless your skill at arms proves you to be stronger and more able than I." The giant dropped his basket and waited; a violent encounter ensued, during which sparks flew from their weapons, but at length Lludd took hold of his opponent, and destiny saw that the victory fell to him as he threw the oppressor to the ground. Having been conquered by force and might, the giant begged for mercy. "How can I grant mercy in view of the number of losses and wrongs you have inflicted upon me?" said Lludd. "I will make good every loss," said the giant, "and I will commit no further outrages, but will be your faithful follower hereafter." Lludd accepted this. Thus Lludd rid the island of the three plagues, ruling it peacefully and prosperously as long as he lived.

—WALES, 14TH CENTURY

The Annals of Ulster, *the chronicle history of Ireland, is filled with passages that recount death, pillage, and fierce violence on the battlefield. In the following entry, we see just how commonplace dying and killing for one's country was during one day in Ireland's history.*

Kalends of (Jan. on 4th feria, 9th of the moon, A.D. 1102. Sort of Colum-cille was burned.—Donnchadh, son of Echri Ua Aitidh, royal heir of the Ui-Eachach, was killed by the Ulidians (namely, in the fifth month after the profaning of Patrick by him).—Domnall, son of Tigernan Ua Ruairc, king of Conmaicni, was killed by the Conmaicni themselves.—Cumhaighi Ua Cairill, herenagh of Dun, died.—Flaithbertach Mac Fothaigh, king of Ui-Fiacrach of Ard-sratha, was killed by the men of Lurg.—A hosting by the Cenel-Eogain to Magh-Coba. The Ulidians went in the night into the camp, so that they killed Sitriuc Ua Mael-fhabhaill (namely, King of Carraic-Brachaide) and Sitriuc, son of Conrach, son of Eogan and others.—Maghnus, king of Lochlann, went with a large fleet into Manann and peace of a year was made by them and by the Men of Ireland. The hostages of the men of Ireland [were placed] in custody of Domnall, successor of

[St.] Patrick, for [securing] peace of a year between Ua Briain
(that is, Muircertach) and Ua Loch-lainn (namely, Domnall) and
so on. Muiredhach Ua Cirdubain, herenagh of Lughbadh, was
killed by the Men of Meath also.—Ross-ailithir (namely, with its
superior) was pillaged by the Ui-Echach [of Munster], in revenge
of the killing of Ua Donnchadha, namely, of Mac-na-her-
luime.—Cashel was burned by the Eili.—Mughron Ua Morghair,
archlector of Ard-Macha and of all the West of Europe, felici-
tously finished his life (namely, in Mungarit) before many witnesses, on [Sunday] the 3rd of the Nones [5th] of October.

—IRELAND, C. A.D.1102

From *The Bruce:*

This selection from the epic Scottish poem The Bruce *warns that
while heroism is critical to the content of one's character, it must
also be married with good judgment. In the verses entitled* On
Valour, *John Barbour gives us a sense of how Robert the Bruce
used both prudence and boldness to overcome the British, and gain
an independent Scotland.*

AH! Valour is a perfect crown!
It leads a man to high renown
If it be followed constantly.
But fame for valour certainly
Is hard to win. For great travail,
Oft to defend, and oft assail.
Yet to be prudent just the same,
Is needful to win valour's fame.
And yet to none will valour serve
Unless good judgment he observe,
And see what is to leave or do.
Extremes there are in valour, two.

The first of these is recklessness;
The other is but cowardice;
And he that wins must both forsake.
For recklessness will undertake
Things that were better left undone;
But cowardice will venture none,
And all and everything forsake.

This will as much for failure make
As over-confidence. Therefore
Does valour merit fame the more
That lies half-way between the two;
And does what it is wise to do,
And leaves what should be left. For it
Inclines to neither opposite,
But uses judgment, that it may
The risk against the advantage weigh.
I am to boldness much inclined
If prudence still be kept in mind.
For foolish boldness is a sin.
But boldness that is woven in
With sense is valour; certainly
Without it, valour cannot be.
This noble king of whom I tell
Mixed prudence with his boldness well,
As ye from this affair may guess.
His wisdom chose the narrow place
And steep ascent beside the ford;
For there, he reckoned, with a sword
A sturdy man might stop the way.
And then his boldness, as I say,
Thought the encounter might be won,
Since they could come one by one.

Thus boldness governed well by wit,
That he would ay together knit,
Earned for his valour lasting fame.
'Twas thus his foes he overcame.

—SCOTLAND, 14TH CENTURY

Beauty

"They are exceedingly careful of cleanliness and neatness, nor in all the country . . . could any man or woman, however poor, be seen either ragged or dirty."
—Ammianus Marcellinus on the Gaul's
belief in physical attractiveness

In the Celtic world, the importance of physical magnificence manifested itself in all areas of life, from mythology to war to literature. The Celts saw physical beauty as a form of exultation and as an escape from the mundane. The emphasis on appearance in the Celtic world was first observed by the classical writers like Polybius, who proclaimed: "Need I speak of the . . . stature and good looks of the people." Lucillius asserted, "They were a beautiful sight, with colorful cloaks and pants and huge torques on their necks." Caesar reported that the Celts were the first people to invent a form of the spa, and Strabo commented on their absolute dedication to staying fit: "The Celts are very careful not to become fat or potbellied. If any young man's belly sticks over his belt, he is punished."

In literature, the importance of beauty in the Celtic world is especially apparent in the descriptions of warriors and gods. In the Celtic hero, beauty has many forms—grace, nobility, a gentle nature, and strength are just as crucial to one's beauty as marble skin or a perfect form. As Nora Chadwick and Miles Dillon observe in their book, *The Celtic Realms,* "Irish gods are always pictured as beautiful in appearance and gloriously dressed." This physical ideal of heroes and gods is always described in the same terms; the truly beautiful—both male and female—always possess white skin, fair hair, nobility of bearing, blue eyes, and impeccable dress. We also see this ideal represented throughout Celtic art from the La Tène period up to the time of the *Book of Kells*—the illuminated manuscript chronicling the four Gospels—in which even Jesus and the Apostles reflect the Celtic idea of beauty; they all possess red or blond hair, blue eyes, and fair skin. Here, as in all forms of their literature and art, we begin to understand the Celtic belief that to be beautiful and glorious in appearance was to be close to God.

In the eighth century Irish saga, The Wooing of Étain, *King Eochaid Airem is enamored of the heroine Étain because she epitomizes the ideal in female beauty. This selection describes all the qualities that define beauty in the Celtic world. We also see the splendid fashion that was characteristic of Celtic dress during this period.*

And Eochaid set forth to take the maiden, and the way that he went across was the fair-green of Bri Leith. And there he saw a maiden upon the brink of a spring. She held in her hand a comb of silver decorated with gold. Beside her, as for washing, was a basin of silver whereon were chased four golden birds, and there were little bright gems of carbuncle set in the rim of the basin. A cloak pure purple, hanging on folds about her, and beneath it a mantle with silver borders, and a brooch of gold in the garment over her bosom. A tunic with a long-hood about her, and as for it, smooth and glossy. It was made of greenish silk beneath red embroidery of gold, and marvelous bow-pins of silver and gold upon her breasts in the tunic, so that the redness of the gold against the sun in the green silk was clearly visible to the men. Two tresses of golden hair upon her head, and a plaiting of four strands in each tress, and a ball of gold upon the end of each plait. And the maiden was there loosening her hair to wash it, and her two arms out through the armholes of her smock. As white as the snow of one night was each of her two arms, and as the red as the fox-glove of the mountain was each of her two cheeks. As blue as the hyacinth was each of her two eyes; delicately red her lips; very high, soft, and white her two shoulders. Tender, smooth, and white were her two wrists; her fingers long and very white; her nails pink and beautiful. As white as snow or as the foam of a wave was her side, slender, long, and as soft as silk. Soft, smooth, and white were her thighs; round and small, firm and white were her two knees; straight as a rule were her two ankles; slim and foam white were her two feet. Fair and very beautiful were her two eyes; her eyebrows blackish blue like the shell of beetle. It was she the maiden who was the fairest and the most beautiful that the eyes of men had ever seen; and it seemed probable to the king and his companions that she was out of a fairy-mound. This was of the maiden concerning whom is spoken the proverb: "Every lovely form must be tested by Étain, every beauty by the standard of Étain."

—IRELAND, 8TH CENTURY

In the Irish saga The Dream of Oenghus, *the hero of the story falls in love after seeing the vision of a beautiful woman, and becomes sick when he finds he cannot see her again. It is only when he lays eyes on her again that he can be healed. In this selection, we discover the divine power of physical beauty in the Celtic view.*

He spoke to him aside. "Ah unhappy plight!" said Finghin, "you have fallen in love in absence." "You have diagnosed my illness," said Oenghus. "You have fallen into a wretched state and have dared not tell it to anyone," said Finghin. "You are right," said Oenghus; "a beautiful girl came to me, of the loveliest figure in Ireland, and of surprising aspect. She had a lute in her hand, and played it to me every night." "No matter," said Finghin, "it is fated for you to make a match with her."

—IRELAND, 8TH CENTURY

In this selection from Taliesin, *we see the emphasis of physical beauty on one's stature in society, particularly during King Arthur's court of the Round Table, when beauty was as crucial as valor.*

In times past there lived in Penllyn a man of gentle lineage, named Tegid Voel, and his dwelling was in the midst of the lake Tegid, and his wife was called Caridwen. And there was born to him of his wife a son named Morvran ab Tegid, and also a daughter named Creirwy, the fairest maiden in the world was she; and they had a brother, the most ill-favoured man in the world, Avagddu. Now Caridwen his mother thought that he was not likely to be admitted among men of noble birth, by reason of his ugliness, unless he had some exalted merits or knowledge. For it was in the beginning of Arthur's time and of the Round Table.

—WALES, 6TH CENTURY

In the following selection from The Maid in the White Gown *by Chrétien de Troyes, a vavasour comments on the importance of his daughter's beauty as well as her grace to Erec the Knight, one of King Arthur's men.*

"In the whole country is no baron, however mighty, who would not marry my daughter, if I would agree; but I look for better things, and am waiting to see whether God will not grant her greater honor, and Fortune send some king or count to take her away; no count or king beneath the skies need be ashamed of my daughter, who is so fair that her peer is not to be found; beautiful she is, but her goodness is better than her beauty; God never made a girl so wise and brave. When my daughter is at my side, I care not a rush for the world; she is my mirth and my joy, my comfort and my solace, my having and my treasure, and there is nothing I love so dearly as herself."

—FRANCE, C. A.D. 1140

From Ailech I:

In this poem from The Dindshenchas, *we see Saint Colum Cille lauded for his physical beauty.*

Colum Cille of the race of Niall,
exceeding pure bright strong with beauty,
even he is a prince for all Scotland, golden diadem of fair
Daire Calgach.

—IRELAND, C. A.D. 1150

In the following quotes from The Mabinogion, *we see that warriors are either rewarded for their beauty or punished for their unattractiveness.*

No man struck him at Camlann—because of his beauty everyone thought he was an angel helping.

—ON SANDDEV ANGEL FACE, WARRIOR AND RELATIVE OF
KING ARTHUR, FROM *HOW CULHWCH WON OLWEN*,
WALES, 14TH CENTURY

No man struck him at Camlann—because of his ugliness, everyone thought he was a devil helping, for there was hair on his face like the hair of a stag.

—ON MORVRAN SON OF TEGID, WARRIOR AND RELATIVE OF
KING ARTHUR, FROM *HOW CULHWCH WON OLWEN*,
WALES, 14TH CENTURY

Bravery

"When at daybreak, the Romans saw that the cavalry were alone, they believed the Celts had fled, and hastened in pursuit of the retreating horse; but when they approached the spot where the enemy were stationed, the Celts suddenly lifted their position and fell upon them. The struggle was at first maintained with fury on both sides: but the courage and the superior numbers of the Celts eventually gave them the victory."
—Polybius, on the Celts' brief but glorious victory over the Romans

The bravery of the ancient Celtic warriors has been celebrated in myth, literature, history, and legend for centuries. Caesar, one of their staunchest enemies, was in awe of their sheer daring and skills in warfare, and remarked, "There was a time . . . when the Gauls were superior in valour to the Germans." The image of the Celtic soldier made famous by Polybius's description of the Celt storming naked, without armor, into battle has become one of the most characteristic depictions of this total disregard for fear. According to Barry Cunliffe's classic, *The Ancient Celts*, the Celtic warrior was "ferocious, impetuous, boastful, and mercurial—not a foe to be tangled with lightly."

The most desirable quality in the Celtic heroes, like Cuchulainn and Kei, is their valor in battle. In this aspect of the Celtic character, like so many others, men and women were equal. Female warriors were expected to be just as fearless—and fierce—as their male counterparts. Queen Medb proves to be just as thirsty for battle as any of the other warriors in *The Táin*, and Scathach is the one who teaches Cuchulainn how to be intrepid on the battlefield.

From the *Boyhood Deeds of Cuchulainn, The Táin*:

In The Táin, *the legend of the mighty Cuchulainn, the epitome of valor and courage, is born:*

"He is the one who could have done the deed," answered Fergus. "He it is who could have lopped the tree with one blow from its root, could have killed the four with the quickness wherewith they were killed and could have come to the border with his charioteer."

"Of a truth," spake Ailill, "I heard from ye of this little boy once on a time in Cruachan. What might be the age of this little boy now?" "It is by no means his age that is most formidable in him," answered Fergus.

"Because manful were his deeds, those of that lad, at a time when he was younger than he now is. In his fifth year, he went in quest of warlike deeds among the lads of Emain Macha. In his sixth year he went to learn skill in arms and feats with Scathach and he went to woo Emer; in his seventh year he took arms; in his seventeenth year he is at this time." "How so!" exclaimed Medb." "Is there even more now amongst the Ulstermen one his equal in age that is more redoubtable than he?" "We have not found there a man at arms that is harder, nor a point that is keener, more terrible nor quicker, nor a more blood thirsty wolf, nor a raven more flesh-loving, nor a wilder warrior, nor a match of his age that would reach to third or fourth the likes of Cuchulain."

—IRELAND, 8TH CENTURY

From the *Boyhood Deeds of Cuchulainn, The Táin*:

In this selection, Cathbad the Druid, one of Ireland's religious leaders, recounts the fame and tragedy that accompany a warrior's bravery on the battlefield.

". . . the little boy that takes up arms this day shall be splendid and renowned for deeds in arms above the youths of Erin and the tales of his deeds shall be told forever, but he shall be shortlived and fleeting."

—IRELAND, 8TH CENTURY

From *The Táin:*

In this poem from Táin Bó Cualinge, *Cuillius the charioteer shows that he is as brave as any warrior.*

I swear to the gods
I'll do great deeds
Before these warriors
Driving to triumph
At full force
On slender steeds
With yokes of silver
And golden wheels
To crush kings' heads
My driven steeds
Will take us leaping to victory.

—IRELAND, 8TH CENTURY

From *Bricriu's Feast:*

In the Irish tale Bricriu's Feast, *three of Ulster's bravest warriors—Cuchulainn, Conall, and Loegaire, must compete in a series of tests of courage to determine who is most worthy to receive "the Champion's Portion" of a sumptuous feast prepared by Bricriu of the Bitter Tongue. In the following selection, Bricriu is deciding how far he must go to test each man's valor. Here we understand just how vital one's daring was to one's manhood, and the qualities a warrior had to possess to be considered truly coura-*

geous. In the Celtic world, it was not enough to be brave—one had to be considered the bravest.

"Then Bricriu set himself to think how with the securities that were given for him, he could best manage to set the men of Ulster against each other. After he had been thinking a while, he went over to Laegaire Buadach son of Connad son of Iliath. "All good be with you, Laegaire, winner of battles, you mighty mallet of Bregia, you hot hammer of Meath, you flame-red thunderbolt, what hinders you from getting the championship of Ireland forever?" "If I want it I can get it," said Laegaire. "You will be head of all the champions in Ireland," said Bricriu, "if you do as I advise." "I will do that, indeed," said Laegaire.

"Well," said Bricriu, "if you can get the Champion's Portion at the feast in my house, the championship of Ireland will be yours forever. And the Champion's Portion of my house is worth fighting for," he said, "for it is not the portion of a fool's house. There goes with it a vat of good wine, with room enough in it to hold three of the brave men of Ulster; with that a seven-year-old boar, that has been fed since it was born on no other thing but fresh milk, and fine meal in spring-time, curds and sweet milk in summer, the kernel of nuts and wheat in harvest, beef and broth in the winter; with that a seven-year-old bullock that never had in its mouth, since it was a sucking calf, either heather or twig tops, but only sweet milk and herbs, meadow hay and corn; along with that, five-score wheaten cakes made with honey. That is the Champion's Portion of my house. And since you are yourself the best hero among the men of Ulster," he said, "it is but right to give it to you; and that is my wish, you to get it. And at the end of the day, when the feast is spread out, let your chariot driver rise up, and it is to him the Champion's Portion will be given." "There will be dead men if that is not done," said Laegaire. Then Bricriu laughed, for he liked to hear that.

When he had done stirring up Laegaire Buadach, he went on to meet with Conall Cearnach. "May good be with you, Conall," he said. "It is you are the hero of fights and of battles; it is many victories you have won up to this over the heroes of Ulster. By the time the men of Ulster cross the boundary of a strange country, it is three days and three nights in advance of them you are, over many a ford and river; it is you who protect their rear coming back again, so that no enemy can get past you or through you, or over you. What would hinder you from being given the Champion's Portion of Emain to hold forever?" Great as was his treachery with Laegaire, he showed twice as much in what he said to Conall Cearnach.

When he satisfied himself that Conall was stirred up to a quarrel, he went on to Cuchulainn. "May all be good with you, Cuchulainn, conqueror of Bregia, bright banner of the Lifé, darling of Emain, beloved by wives and by maidens, Cuchulainn is no nickname for you to-day, for you are the champion of the men of Ulster; it is you keep off their great quarrels and disputes; it is you get justice for every man of them; it is you have what all the men of Ulster are wanting in; all the men of Ulster acknowledge that your bravery, your valour, and your deeds are beyond their own. Why, then, would you leave the Champion's Portion for some other one of the men of Ulster, when not one of them would be able to keep it from you?"

"By the god of my people," said Cuchulainn, "whoever comes to try and keep it from me will lose his head."

—IRELAND, 8TH CENTURY

From How Culhwch Won Olwen:

In this selection from the Welsh Mabinogion, *Kei, a knight of King Arthur's court, displays all of the bravery and prowess that were required of a renowned warrior.*

He had this talent: nine days and nine nights his breath would last under water, and nine days and nine nights he could go without sleep. No doctor could cure the wound from Kei's sword. He could be as tall as the tallest tree in the forest when he pleased, while when the rain was heaviest a hand's span about what was in his hand would be dry by reason of the heat he generated, and when his companions were coldest that would be kindling for the lighting of a fire.

—WALES, 14TH CENTURY

Death

"The cardinal doctrine which they seek to teach is that souls do not die, but after death pass from one to another; and this belief, as the fear of death is thereby cast aside, they hold to be the greatest incentive to valour."

—Caesar, on the Celtic view of death, from *The Gallic War*

Just as the ancient Celts were fearless in life, they were fearless in the face of death. A noble death was just as important as a glorious life. As Lucan observed, they saw death as "only a pause in a long life," an intriguing rite of passage, in which the soul could be reborn. In the Celtic world, death was seen as a natural part of the cycle of life, and paved the way for the journey to the Otherworld, where healing and renewal could begin.

This respect and reverence for death can be seen in the superb tombs at Hallstadt, which were wildy ornate and amply supplied with provisions for the dead to take into the next life. Tertullian confirmed this view when he wrote of their funeral practices: "It is often said because of visions in dreams, the dead truly live. . . . The Celts for the same reason spend the night near the tombs of their famous men." And Caesar was also awed by their ceremony in honoring the dead and paving their way for the next life: "The funerals, considering the civilization of Gaul, are magnificent and expensive."

This complete security in the belief in life after death is particularly evident in Celtic literature, particularly in the Arthurian legends. This faith in the life of the soul after the death of the body is best represented by birds in Celtic legend. Ravens and crows were believed to be messengers from the Otherworld and their cries were thought to signal the death of the person who heard them. In *The Mabinogion*, Lleu does not die, but is transformed into an eagle, while Arthur assumes the shape of a raven. Throughout Celtic literature, from Scottish poetry to Welsh legends, one common truth runs throughout: Death is an inevitability to be embraced and understood, not feared—no matter what form it takes or how it is represented.

> *In the death tales of the Ulster heroes, warriors meet their mortality willingly, even when they are certain of their end. In* The Death of Cuchulainn, *the Irish hero enters fearlessly into battle against Lugaid and the enemies of Ulster, despite an ominous prophecy from the Morrigan, goddess of death and battle. She even goes so far as to break his chariot to prevent him from going to fight, as she knows that if he does, he will never return home to Emain Macha. But even this does not deter him. In the following selection, we see Cuchulainn as the personification of courage in the face of death.*

Then Erc son of Cairbre took the spear: "What shall fall by this spear, O sons of Catalin?" said Erc son of Cairbre.

"Not hard to say: a king falls by that spear," said the sons of Catalin.

"I heard you say that a king would fall by that spear which Lugain long since cast."

"And that is true," said the sons of Catalin. "Thereby fell the king of the charioteers of Erin, namely Cuchulain's charioteer, Loeg mac Riangabra."

Now Erc cast the spear at Cuchulainn, and it lighted on his horse, the Gray of Macha. Cuchulainn snatched out the spear. And each of them bade each other farewell. Threat the Gray of Macha left him with half the yoke under his neck and went into the Gray's Linn in Sliab Fuait.

Thereupon Cuchulainn again drove through the host and was the third pair contending, and he intervened as he had done before, and the satirist demanded his spear, and Cuchulainn at first refused it.

"I will revile thee," said the satirist.

"I have paid for my honor today. I am not bound to grant more than one request this day."

"I will revile Ulster for thy fault."

"I have paid for Ulster's honor," said Cuchulainn.

" I will revile thy race," said the satirist.

"Tidings that I have been defamed shall never reach the land I have not reached. For little there is of my life remaining."

So Cuchulainn flung the spear to him, handle foremost, and it went through his head and through thrice nine other men.

"'Tis grace with wrath, O Cuchulainn," said the satirist.

Then Cuchulainn for the last time drove through the host, and Lugaid took the spear and said: "What will fall by this spear, O sons of Catalin?"

"I heard you say that a king would fall by the spear that Erc cast this morning."

"That is true," said they, "the king of the steeds of Erin fell by it, namely the Gray of Macha."

Then Lugain flung the spear and struck Cuchulainn, and his bowels came forth on the cushion of the chariot, and his only horse, the Black Sainglenn, fled away, with half the yoke hanging to him, and left the chariot and his master, the king of the heroes of Erin, dying alone on the plain.

Then said Cuchulainn, "I would fain go as far as that loch to drink a drink thereout."

"We give thee leave," said they, "provided that thou come to us again."

"I will bid you come for me," said Cuchulainn, "if I cannot come myself." Then he gathered his bowels into his breast, and went forth to the loch. And there he drank his drink, and washed himself, and came forth to die, calling on his foes to come meet him.

Now a great mearing went westwards from the loch and his eye lit upon it, and he went to a pillar-stone which is in the plain, and he put his breast-girdle round it that he might not die seated nor lying down, but that he might die standing up. Then came the men all around him, but they durst not go to him, for they thought he was alive.

—IRELAND, 8TH CENTURY

This selection from The Death of Arthur *by Chrétien de Troyes depicts the final end of King Arthur as one that every Celtic hero aspired to—brave, noble, and at the hands of a worthy opponent. In this case, Arthur's opponent is his own nephew, Mordred, who has committed adultery with his wife, Guinevere, and who has claimed Arthur's kingdom as his own—the ultimate treachery. This passage is also characteristic of the Celtic belief that death is never the final end, as we discover when Arthur is mortally wounded in battle and journeys to the Otherworld, called Avalon, to be healed.*

Arthur started on his steed, naught could understand him. Mordred was wild with rage, and leapt into his saddle; no more of truce, but they featured spears and rushed together. Mordred marred many a man, and rode through many a rank; and Arthur

ceased not to deal cruel wounds, from morn when the fray began,
till night fell; many a shield was shivered and curse cried, many a
brand bent and helm broken. The hosts ran together, a hundred
thousand strong; since Brutus parted from Troy, and in Britain
made his home, never were such wonders wrought. By even, on
that field remained no living man, save Mordred alone, and
Arthur with two of his knights, Lucan the butler, bleeding of
many wound, and his brother Sir Bedivere, sick and infirm.

Arthur cried, "Shall we not bring down this thief?" A spear
he gript, and they ran together; Mordred he struck in the breast,
so that the point came out at the back, and he spake no more; as
he fell, he lifted his head and through helm and crest smote the
king, that thrice he swooned. Between them Sir Lucan and Sir
Bedivere sustained the king; together they quitted the field, that
was covered with slain. To a chapel they turned, for they wist not
what better to do; all night they lay in that chapel by the sea, crying mercy to Mary, with dreary heart and woeful voice, and to her
dear son they prayed: "Jesu, for thy seven names, show his soul the
right way, that he lose not heavenly bliss!"

As Sir Lucan gazed from a height, he saw bold barons, who
robbed from the dead of bezants and rings; to the king he returned, and warned him with words: "Sir, from yon hill have I
seen folk draw to the downs; I wot not if they mean evil or good;
let us make ready, and wend to a town." "As thou sayest: Sir
Lucan, lift me, while my life may last." The king embraced him
with all his might; he was weak with loss of blood, and swooned as
he looked down; Sir Lucan was hard bested; he held the king till
his own heart broke. When the king came to himself, he stood beside an altar; Sir Lucan, whom he loved, lay afoam in his blood;
his brother Sir Bedivere would not come nigh, but wept as if he
were wild. The king turned to Sir Bedivere, with keen words:
"Take Excalibur, my good sword, better brand was never seen; go,

cast it in the salt flood, and I ween, wonders shalt thou behold. Hie thee, for cross on rood, and bring word what thou hast seen."

The knight was fain to save that good sword: "What gain if one own it? 'Twere madness to throw it in the flood." He hid it under a tree, and returned. "Sir, I did as you bade." "What sawest thou there? Tell me, if thou canst." "Certes, sir, naught save waters deep and waves wan." "Ah, thou hast broken my hest! False man, why hast thou so done? Other tidings must thou bring."

The knight ran, and thought to hide the sword, and cast the scabbard in the sea: "If aught strange befalleth, some token shall I perceive." He let the sheath sink, and a while stood on the land; to the king he went: "Sir, by the rood, 'tis done." "Sawest thou marvels more?" "Certes, sir, naught." "Ah, false traitor! Twice hast thou wrought treason; be sure it shall cost thee dear." Sir Bedivere cried: "Lord, thy mercy!" and cast the brand into the sea; then might he know what the king meant; from the water came a hand and seized the sword, brandishing it as if it would break, and glinted away like a gleam.

He went back and said: "Sir, I saw a hand; it came from the water, and thrice brandished that royal sword." "Help me, that I wend thither." Sir Bedivere guided his lord to the shore, where lay a fair ship, full of ladies; she that was brightest of beauty wept and wrung her hands: "Brother, woe is me; from healing hast thou been too long, alas for thy cruel pangs!" The knight made a woeful cry: "Lord, whither are you bound? Alas, whither away?" With a sad voice spake the king: "For a while will I go to the vale of Avalon, there to be healed of my wound."

—FRANCE, C. A.D. 1170

In this quote from the Arthurian legend The Disinherited Damsel *by Chrétien de Troyes, death takes a human form. Here we see that death always has the upper hand; and is a certainty that must be obeyed, not avoided.*

Meantime, Death had so argued with the Lord of the Black Thorn that needs must he die; after he had departed, the elder of his two daughters declared that she would have the whole of the estate, and her sister should get no part.

—FRANCE, C. A.D. 1170

Eloquence

"The Gauls have a fearsome appearance and deep rough voices. They are a people of few words and often speak in riddles, leaving many things for the listener to understand himself. They love exaggeration both to praise themselves and belittle others. They are boastful, threatening, and love melodramatic behavior, but also have sharp minds and are quick learners. They have singing poets called bards who perform playing an instrument like a Greek lyre. These bards sing songs of praise and of satire."

—Diodorus Siculus on the Celtic love of language

Because it was the eighth century A.D. before the ancient Celts began to write most of their stories down, the power of the spoken word was crucial to them and cherished above all else. The classical historians like Strabo confirmed that the Bards, ancient poets blessed with golden tongues, were one of the three most honored groups according to Celtic law, along with the Druids and the Vates. Lucian best summed up the Celtic love affair with words in his report of his conversation with a Celt regarding the true definition of eloquence:

We Celts do not agree with you Greeks that Hermes represents eloquence. We think instead that the power of the spoken word is best shown by Hercules, since he is much stronger. And don't be surprised that we portray him as an old man. Eloquence is most likely to show itself in the fullness of age, not in youth. . . . So if we see old Hercules here leading men away by his tongue, don't be surprised. Our common tradition here is that Hercules achieved most of his great deeds by using the power of words. I suppose the arrows in his quiver represent words—sharp, fast, and hitting the target—which pierce the spirit of the listener.

The oral tradition of the ancient Celts continues to influence the emphasis of powerful speech and storytelling in Irish, Welsh, and Scottish societies to this day. There was no greater gift than the ability to speak fluently and effectively. In Celtic literature, a clever tongue had the power to outsmart enemies, seduce a lover, gain favor at court, and sing the praises of heroes. For example, in Welsh literature, Gwalchmei disarms his opponents with the power of words, and Kynon, the great storyteller in *The Mabinogion*, affirms his belief that there is nothing worse than "a poor talker." The other characters also display disarming verbal talents. Rhiannon is renowned for her sharp tongue, and Manawydan is able to rescue Pryderi from the Otherworld by bargaining with Llywyd, without the use of force. It is this reverence for the spoken word in ancient Celtic literature that continues to influence the language and literature of modern Celtic nations.

In The Mabinogion, *the great storyteller Kynon from* Owein, *or* The Countess of the Fountain *is the physical manifestation of eloquence:*

"He asked me what sort of errand I was on and what sort of man I was; I answered that it was high time I had someone to talk with, and that at court there was nothing worse than a poor talker."
—WALES, 14TH CENTURY

From *The Mabinogion:*

Gwalchmei armed himself and made for Peredur at his horse's easy gait, and he found the knight leaning on his spear shaft and meditating still. He approached with no sign of hostility and said, "If I thought it would please you as much as me, I would talk to you. I am a messenger from Arthur, who asks you to come and see him. Two men have come before me on this same errand." "That is true," said Peredur, "they came discourteously and fought with me, and I was displeased inasmuch as I disliked being aroused from my meditation. I was thinking of the woman I love best, and this is how I happened to remember her; I was looking at the snow and the raven and the drops of blood from the duck which the hawk killed, and thinking how the whiteness of her skin is like the whiteness of the snow, and the blackness of her hair and eyebrows like the raven, and the two red spots in her cheeks like the two drops of blood." "That was no ignoble meditation, nor was it strange that you disliked being distracted from it," said Gwalchmei. "Tell me, is Kei in Arthur's court?" "He is. He is the last knight you encountered, and he came to grief." He broke his right arm and collar-bone with the fall he took from your spear thrust." "Well, I am not dismayed at having begun to take revenge for the insult to the dwarf and his wife." Gwalchmei was surprised to hear the knight speak of the dwarf and his wife; he drew near Peredur and embraced him and asked what his name was. "I am called Peredur son of Evrawg—who are you?" "I am called Gwalchmei." "I am happy to see you—in every land I have encountered your reputation for strength and loyalty, and I entreat your companionship." "By my faith you shall have that, and give me yours." "Gladly," said Peredur. The two men set out in joyful friendship towards Arthur. When Kei heard them coming he said, "I knew Gwalchmei would not need to fight with the knight, nor is it strange that he has won renown—he has done more with kind words than we by force of arms."

—WALES, 14TH CENTURY

In this selection from The Dean of Lismore, *the poet Duncan Mor from Lenox sings of the importance of eloquence to the Bard:*

Pity the man who lost his voice,
When he is called on to recite,
Who cannot speak so fast as needs be,
And yet's unwilling to give up.
Who cannot sing an air or tune,
And cannot well recite a lay.
Who cannot put aside his harp,
Yet cannot sing as he would wish.
Pity him ever with his "dring, drang,"
Trying his verses to recite,
When men can neither hear his harp,
Nor understand the songs he sings.

—SCOTLAND, 16TH CENTURY

Family

"The Gauls affirm that they are all descended from a common father, Dis, and say that this is the tradition of the Druids. . . . In the other ordinances of life, the main difference between them and the rest of mankind is that they do not allow their own sons to approach them openly until they have grown to an age when they can bear the burden of military service, and they count it a disgrace for a son who is still in his boyhood to take his place publicly in the presence of his father."
—Caesar's observation of the ancient Celtic practice of fosterage

While many scholars who have studied the history of ancient Celtic societies remark on their intense regard for family, it is interesting to note the classical writers' observations on the Celtic family structure. Caesar's observations in *The Gallic Wars* make Gallic parents—particularly fathers—seem harsh and unloving. He also remarks on the Celtic practice of dipping babies in cold water to strengthen their immune systems. However, despite these somewhat iron-fisted descriptions of the ancient Celts, it is clear that they had a deep dedication to family life. Celtic law, particularly the Brehon Laws, devotes a great deal of time and energy to outlining the proper rearing of children. Of the eight laws included in the Law of Social Connections, for example, four make provisions for family relationships, particularly relationships between father and daughter, mother and son, sister and brother, and foster son and foster mother. Also, the "Geilfine" system outlined in the Brehon Laws specifically defines the Irish family organization: a family unit was made up of seventeen members and was led by a "head chief." According to the Law of Fosterage, each child in the community was raised and taught by the other members of the tribe. Fosterage would have been the equivalent of a modern school and was a remarkably enlightened method of child-rearing, by which all members of a community served as an extended family, and which was likely what Caesar was observing when he remarked that fathers would not acknowledge their sons in public. The idea of fosterage also broadened the definition of "family" to extend beyond blood relatives. The members of one's own community could also be considered family members.

In literature, it is clear that love and devotion to one's family is always greatly rewarded, although these relationships can also be fraught. In the Welsh *Mabinogion,* Arthur's allegiance to his family is unshakeable. In the same way, Llevelys seeks the counsel of his brother Lludd and marries a woman who will honor his family. In the ancient Irish sagas, such as *How Ronan Slew His Son,* we see a different side of family life, where love for family can turn sinister.

In the Irish saga How Ronan Slew His Son, *the famous Irish High King Ronan seeks a new wife in the beautiful young daughter of Eochaid, the northern high king. She marries him and becomes his queen, but she really desires Ronan's son, the young and handsome Mael Fothartaig. He refuses her, in loyalty to his father, and in retaliation she tells Ronan that Mael Fothartaig has seduced her. In this selection, we see Mael Fothartaig's loyalty to his father, and in turn we also see Ronan's envy of his young son. It is a classic father-son tale—one of undying devotion, fierce jealousy, and revenge.*

Ronan came home. Mael Forthartaig's men came into the house before him. He stayed alone outside the hunting. "Where is Mael Fothartaig to-night, Congal?" said Ronan.

"He is outdoors," said Congal.

"Woe is me, my son to be abroad alone, and the number to whom he gives good things!"

"You have made us deaf with talking about your son," said his wife.

"It is right to talk of him," said Ronan. "For there is not in Ireland a son better according to the wish of his father. For his jealousy on my behalf is the same with both men and women at Ath Cliath and at Clar Daire Moir and at Drochet Cairbri as if it were for his own soul, so that there is ease for me and for you, woman," said Ronan.

"Truly," she said, "he shall not get from me the ease that he wishes, even to meet with me to your dishonour. I shall not be alive withstanding him any longer. Congal has taken me to him three times since morning, so that I with difficulty escaped from his hands."

"Malediction on your lips, you bad woman!" said Ronan. "It is false."

"You will see a proof of it now," said she. "I will sing half a quatrain to see whether it will fit with what Mael Fothartaig will sing." He used to do this every night to please her. He would sing one half quatrain, she would sing the other half.

He came in then and was drying his shins at the fire, and Congal by his side. His jester MacGlass was at his games on the floor of the house. Then Mael Fothartaig said, for the day was cold:

It is cold against the whirlwind
For any one herding the cows of Aifè.

"Hear this Ronan," said she. "Sing that again," said she.

It is cold against the whirlwind
For any one herding the cows of Aifè.

Said she:

It is a vain herding,
With no kine, with no lover to meet.

(That is, "Neither did I come, nor did you take the cows with you.)

"It is true this time," said Ronan. There was a warrior by Ronan's side, Aedan son of Fiachna Lara. "O Aedan," said he, "a spear into Mael Fothartaig, and another into Congal!" When Mael Fothartaig had turned his back to them by the fire, Aedan planted the spear in him, so that he put its points though him, as he was on his seat. As Congal rose Aedan thrust a spear into him, so that it passed through his heart. The jester jumped up. Aedan sent a spear after him so it brought his bowels out.

"You have wrought enough on the men, O Aedan!" said Mael Fothartaig from his seat.

"It was your luck," said Ronan, "that you found no woman to solicit but my wife."

"Wretched is that falsehood, O Ronan," said the youth, "which has been put on you to kill your only son without guilt. By your rank and by the tryst to which I go, the tryst with death, not greater is my guilt to think of meeting with her than that I should meet with my mother. But she has been soliciting me since she came into the land, and Congal has taken her back three times today that she might not meet me. There was no guilt in Congal that you should kill him." Then a raven carried the bowels of the jester on the front-bridge . . . of the stronghold. The churls were laughing. Mael Fothartaig thought it a villainy. He said:

O Mac Glass
Gather your bowels in,

Though you know no shame,
Churls are laughing at you.

Thereafter the three died. They were taken into a house apart. Ronan went and sat at the head of his son three days and three nights.

—IRELAND, 12TH CENTURY

In this selection from The Mabinogion, *Llevelys chooses family love over romantic love when choosing a wife.*

Beli the Great, son of Mynogan, had three sons: Lludd and Casswallawn and Nynnyaw, and according to this story there was a fourth son, Llevelys. After Beli's death the kingdom of Britain passed into the hands of the eldest son Lludd, and Lludd ruled it prosperously. He rebuilt the walls of London and surrounded the city with innumerable towers, and then he ordered its inhabitants to build houses such as no other kingdom possessed. Moreover, he was a good fighter, and generous and open-handed in giving food and drink to all who sought them. Though he had many strong-holds and fortresses he loved London best; he spent most of the year there, and so it was called Caer Lludd, later Caer Llundein, though after the foreigners came it was called Lundein or Lwndrwy. Of his brothers Lludd loved Llevelys best, for the latter was both handsome and wise. When Llevelys heard that the king of France had died and left a daughter as his only heir, putting the kingdom in her hands, he went to ask advice and help of his brother Lludd, not so much for his own advantage as to seek to augment the honour and dignity and worth of their family by going to France and asking the girl to be his wife. Lludd was of the same opinion, so that Llevelys was glad to take his advice; at once ships were fitted out and nobles brought aboard and they set out for France. Upon their arrival messengers were sent to inform the French nobles of their errand, whereupon the nobles and princes held a council and decided to give Llevelys both the girl and the crown of their realm. Thereafter Llevelys ruled with honesty and dignity, as long as he lived.

—WALES, 14TH CENTURY

In this selection from Chrétien de Troyes' The Quest Of the Holy Grail, *Lancelot discovers his deep family attachment to Galahad. We also see how important family ties were during the time of Arthur's court, and we understand the idea of fosterage at work within the Knights of the Round Table. Family was not just defined by love, but also by affection and deep friendship.*

In Camelot, on Whitsuneve, after the companions of the Round Table had returned from the service, the tables were set. At nones, rode in the hall a lady, who had ridden in such haste that her palfrey was all of foam. She dismounted, and stood before the king, whom she saluted, and asked if Lancelot of the Lake were present. "Aye," answered the king, "in this hall," and he pointed him out. The damsel went to Lancelot's seat, and said: "Lancelot, in the name of King Pelles, I bid you attend me to yonder forest." He demanded whom she might be. "I belong," she said, "to whom I have named." "And what would you of me?" "You shall learn," she said. "I will go," he returned, "so that it be in the name of God." With that Lancelot bade a squire saddle his steed, and fetch his arms; when the king and the barons heard, they were disturbed, but perceived that there was no help. The queen inquired wherefore he quitted them on so holy a day; but the damsel said they should have him on the morrow, before the dinner hour. Lancelot mounted, together with the damsel, and set out unattended, save by a single squire, who had brought her to Camelot.

When they reached the forest, they followed a high road, and proceeded until they came to a vale; at a cross, they saw before them an abbey, whither rode the damsel, as fast as her horse could carry her. When they reached the gate, the squire called, and they were admitted; Lancelot was received with joy, and conducted to a chamber, where he was disarmed. Asleep in two beds he found his cousins, Bors and Lionel, and awakened them; they embraced him with delight, and asked what chance had brought him from Camelot. Lancelot related how he had been summoned, wherefore he whist not; as they conversed, entered three nuns, leading Galahad, a child, so fair that scarce could his equal be found. She who seemed highest in rank held him by the hand, weeping tenderly. "Sir," she said, "I bring you our nursling, our comfort and hope, that you may make him a knight." Lancelot gazed at the youth, and found him so furnished with all beauty that he had never seen aught equally fair; he answered that their request should be granted. "Sir," said they, "in God's name," he responded, "as you will."

That night Lancelot remained in the abbey, and caused the youth to keep his vigil in the church; on the morrow, at prime, he made him knight. He himself shod on one of the spurs, and Bors the other; after that, Lancelot gave him the accolade, praying that God might make him worthy, for beauty had he sufficient. When Lancelot had finished, he said: "Fair sir, attend me to the court of King Arthur." "Sir," replied Galahad, "with you I will not go." "Lady," cried Lancelot to the abbess, "Suffer your new knight to accompany me to the court of the king, where he will be of more service than here with you." "Sir," she answered, "not now, but we will send him when it shall be time."

Lancelot and his cousins took leave, and rode until they came to Camelot, at the hour of tierce, when the king had gone to the monastery to hear mass. They ascended to the hall, and began to talk of the fair child whom Lancelot had knighted; and Bors said that he had never seen anyone who so marvellously resembled Lancelot. "Indeed," he cried, 'I will never guess again, if it be not Galahad, whom Lancelot begot from the fair daughter of King Pelles, for he hath the feature of that line, and of our own." Lionel answered, that it was very likely; so they said, to see whether they could move Lancelot to speak, but he uttered no word.

When they ceased talking, they inspected the seats of the Round Table, and on each found inscribed the name of the knight who belonged to that place. As they came to the Siege Perilous, they saw letters which ran: "From the passion of Christ are fulfilled years four hundred and fifty-four, and on Whitsunday of this present year shall this seat find its lord." They exclaimed, that the adventure was strange; and Lancelot declared, none should read the legend, until the arrival of the man who was destined to accomplish the prediction; so speaking, he covered the chair with a silken cloth. After the king had returned from mass, and knew that Lancelot had arrived, with Lionel and Bors, he made much of them, and the Knights of the Round Table were merry over the advent of the three comrades. The king bade the tables be set, but Kei cried: "Sir, if you sit at meat, you will infringe the custom of the house, for on so holy a day it is not your wont to dine, until some adventure be reported at your court." The king replied that Kei had spoken the truth, but he had forgotten the rule, because of his joy in the arrival of Lancelot and his mates.

—FRANCE, C. 1140–1200

Friendship

In the Celtic world, even when friends are locked in mortal combat, they show an undying love for one another. This is especially apparent in the Irish epic *The Táin*. Cuchulainn declares unconditional love to his friend Ferdiad, who will later become one of his fiercest enemies. Even in combat, Cuchulainn mourns his death and declares their battle shameful. Same-sex friendships are especially prevalent in *The Táin* as well as in Arthurian legends. The love one man has for another can often be as strong as the love he feels for a lover.

In the Welsh epic *The Mabinogion*, Pwyll is rewarded for his friendship towards Arawn with treasure beyond his wildest dreams, and Manawydan and Pryderi enjoy a friendship that is so strong that neither can be without the other. In the Celtic epic, a friend is a friend for life—even in the fiercest struggle.

From *The Táin:*

The friendship between Ferdiad and Cuchulainn is one of the most passionate—and the most fraught—in Celtic literature. Soul mates since their youth, they were both trained in arms by Scathach and were fierce warriors. Queen Medb beguiles Ferdiad into fighting Cuchulainn in an attempt to destroy her mortal enemy. In these selections from The Tain, *we see how a fierce friendship becomes a fierce battle:*

From *The Táin:*

Cuchulain: we were heart companions once;
We were comrades in the woods;
We were men that shared a bed,
When we slept a heavy sleep
After hard and weary fights,
Into many lands so strange
Side by side we sallied forth
And we ranged the woodlands through,
When with Scathach we learned arms!

—IRELAND, 8TH CENTURY

From *The Táin:*

"Verily it is truly meant for thee." said Cuchulainn, "for comes there a brace of birds into the plain, thou shall have a wild goose with half the other. If fish rise to the river-mouths to the stones or water falls thou shalt have a salmon with as much again. Thou shalt have a handful of watercress and a handful of seagrass . . . I will watch and guard thee as long as thou sleepest."

—IRELAND, 8TH CENTURY, CUCHULAINN TO FERGUS,
FROM *THE DEATH OF ETARCOMOL*

From *The Táin:*

Food has not passed his lips,
Nay, nor has yet been born,
Son of king or blameless queen,
For whom I would work thee harm.

—IRELAND, 8TH CENTURY , CUCHULAINN TO FERDIAD,
THE COMBAT OF FERDIAD AND CUCHULAINN

From *The Táin:*

Alas, golden brooch
Ferdiad of the hosts
O good smiter, strong victories thy hand.

Your hair blond and curled,
Like a lovely jewel,
Thy soft-shaped belt
Around thee till death.

Our Comradeship dear;
Thy noble eye's gleam
Thy golden rimmed shield
Thy sword treasures worth!

To fall by my hand I own was not just!
'Twas no noble fight.
Alas, golden brooch!

> —IRELAND, 8TH CENTURY, CUCHULAINN ON HIS GREAT FRIEND
> AND ENEMY, FERDIAD, FROM *THE COMBAT OF FERDIAD AND
> CUCHULAINN*

From *The Mabinogion:*

*The friendship between the Welsh king Pywll and Arawn, King
of Annwvyn is one of the richest and most loyal in Welsh literature. In this selection from from* Pwyll, Lord of Dyved, *we see
how Pwyll's undying devotion to Arawn is both tested and rewarded.*

Pwyll, Lord of Dyved ruled over the seven cantrevs of that
land. One day, when he was in his chief court at Arberth, his
thoughts and desires turned to hunting. Glynn Cuch was the part

of his realm he wanted to hunt, so he set out that evening from Arberth and went as far as Penn Llwyn on Bwya, where he spent the night. At dawn the next day he rose and made for Glynn Cuch, in order to turn his hounds loose in the forest; he blew his horn and began to muster the hunt, but in riding after the hounds he became separated from his companions. As he listened to the baying of his pack he perceived the cry of another pack, a different cry which was advancing towards him. He spied a clearing in the forest, a level field, and as his pack reached the edge of this field he saw the other pack with a stag running before it, and near the centre of the clearing this other pack overtook the stag and brought it down. Pwyll at once remarked the pack's colour, without bothering to look at the stag, for no hound he had ever seen was the colour of these: a dazzling shining white with red ears, and as the whiteness of the dogs shone so did the redness of their ears. Even so he approached and drove off the strange hounds and baited his own upon the stag.

As Pwyll was about this he saw beyond the other pack a rider approaching on a great dapple-gray horse, wearing a hunting horn round his neck and a hunting dress of grayish-brown material. This horseman rode up to him and said, "Chieftain, I know who you are, but I will not greet you." "Well," replied Pwyll, "perhaps your rank prevents your doing so." "God knows, it is not the degree of my rank which prevents me." "What else, chieftain?" asked Pwyll. "Between me and God," said the stranger, "your own rudeness and discourtesy." "Chieftain, what discourtesy have you seen in me?" "In no man have I seen greater discourtesy than driving away the pack which has killed a stag and baiting one's own pack upon it. That was your discourtesy, and though I will take no vengeance, between me and God, I will dishonour you to the value of a hundred stags." "Chieftain," said Pwyll, "if I have done wrong, I will earn your friendship." "How?" asked the other. "As befits your rank—only I do not know who you are." "I am a crowned king in my own land." "Lord, good day to you," said Pwyll. "What land do you come from?" "Annwvyn," said the other. "I am Arawn, King of Annwvyn." "Lord, how can I earn your friendship?" "This is how," said Arawn. "There is a man— Havgan, King of Annwvyn, whose realm borders on mine, and he is constantly waging war against me. By ridding me of his oppression, which you can do easily, you will earn my friendship." "I will do that gladly," said Pwyll, "only tell me how I can." "That I will," said Arawn. "We will make a strong bond of friendship. I will send you into Annwvyn in my place, and give you the loveliest woman you have ever seen to sleep with every night; moreover I will endow you with my shape and appearance so that no chamberlain, no officer, no follower of mine will know that you are not I. All this for a year and a day, and then we will meet again here." "Fair enough," said Pwyll. "But even if I stay in your land for a year, how am I to find the man of whom you speak?" "A year from tonight," said Arawn, "he and I are to meet at the ford. You will be there in my place; strike him one blow, which he will not survive, and if he asks you to finish him off hold your hand, no matter how much he begs you. For however often I struck him, the next day he would be fighting as well as before." "Very well," said Pwyll, "but what will I do with my own kingdom?" "I will see that neither man nor woman knows that I am not you, for I will go in your place." "Then I will be glad to go." "Your journey will be free of trouble; nothing will impede your progress to my kingdom; for I myself will guide you." Arawn then led Pwyll to where they could see the court and the other dwellings. "This court and kingdom are now yours. Make straight for the court; no one there will fail to recognize you, and as you observe people's behaviour you will learn our customs."

Pwyll rode towards the court, and once inside he saw dwellings and hails and chambers and the finest assembly of buildings anyone had seen. He entered the hall to change; youths and servants appeared and pulled off his boots, and each one greeted Pwyll as he went by. Two horsemen came to remove his hunting garb and clothe him in a garment of gold brocade. Then the hall was made ready; he could see troops and companies entering, the finest looking and best equipped troops anyone had seen, and with them the queen, dressed in shining gold brocade, the most beautiful woman anyone had seen. Everyone washed and went to sit down; the queen sat on one side of Pwyll, and the earl (so he surmised) on the other. Pwyll began to talk to his queen, and of all the women he had ever talked with, she was the least affected, and most gracious in disposition and conversation. They passed the time eating and drinking and singing and carousing, and of all the courts he had ever seen, this was the best supplied with golden plate and royal jewels: When it was time to sleep Pwyll and his queen went to bed, and as soon as they were in the bed he turned his face to the edge and his back to her, nor did he speak another word before morning. The next day tenderness and affectionate conversation were resumed, but however affectionate they were by day, not one night during the following year was different from the first one.

Pwyll spent that year hunting and singing and carousing, in fellowship and in pleasant talk with his companions, up to the night of the meeting, which the men in the most distant parts of the kingdom remembered as well as he did himself. He was accompanied by the nobles of the realm, and as they reached the ford a horseman rose and said, "Nobles, listen well. This encounter lies between the two kings, in single combat, for each one claims the land and the domain of the other; therefore let everyone else stand back." With that the two kings drew near and met in the middle of the ford. On the first rush the man who was in Arawn's place struck Havgan's shield in the centre of the boss so that it split into two halves; Havgan's armour shattered, and he himself was thrown an arm and a spear's length over his horse's hindquarters to the ground, where he lay mortally wounded. "Chieftain," he said, "what right did you have to kill me? I made no claim against you, nor do I know of any reason why you should kill me. But since you have begun so, finish me off now." "Chieftain, I may yet regret doing to you what I have done. He who wishes to may strike you again, but I will not." "Loyal followers," said Havgan, "carry me away, for my end is now certain, and I can no longer maintain you." "Sirs," said the man who was in Arawn's place, "talk among yourselves and decide who ought to be my men," and they answered, "Lord, all men ought to be, for there is over Annwvyn no king but yourself." "Good. Let those who offer their submission be received, and those who are unwilling be compelled by the sword." Thus he received the homage of the men and began to rule the land, and by noon of the following day both realms were in his power.

Pwyll then set out for the meeting-place. He made for Glynn Cuch, and when he arrived Arawn was there waiting for him, and each was glad to see the other. "God reward your friendship," said Arawn. "Well," said Pwyll, "when you arrive in your own land, you will see what I have done for you." "For what you have done, God reward you." Then Arawn restored Pwyll's shape and appearance, and took back his own, so that each man was himself again.

Arawn set out for his court in Annwvyn, and he was happy to see the companies and troops which he had missed for so long; they however knew nothing of his absence, and his arrival was no greater novelty than it had ever been. He spent the day in pleasure and merrymaking, in sitting and talking with his wife and his nobles, and when it was time to sleep rather than to carouse they went to bed. Arawn got into the bed and his wife came to him, and at once he began to talk to her, to hold her and caress her lovingly. She had not been so treated for the past year, and she thought, "My God, how different he is tonight from what he has been." She thought a long time; he woke, and spoke to her, a second time, and even a third, but she gave no answer. "Why do you not answer me?" he asked, whereupon she said, "I tell you that for a year now I have not spoken at all in this place." "How can that be? We have always talked in bed." "Shame on me," she said, "if since a year from yesternight this bed has seen conversation or pleasure between us, or even your turning your face to me, let alone anything more." That set Arawn to thinking. "Lord God," he said, "what a faithful comrade I took for a friend." Then he said to his wife, "Lady, do not blame me, for I have neither lain down nor slept with you this past year." He told her what had happened, and she said, "I confess to God, you made a strong pact for your friend to have fought off the temptations of the flesh and kept faith with you." "Lady, that was my thought when I was silent." "No wonder," she said.

Meanwhile Pwyll, Lord of Dyved arrived in his own realm and country, and began to question his nobles as to how he had ruled the past year compared with previous ones. They answered, "Lord, never have you been so perceptive, nor so kind; never have you distributed your goods more freely, never was your discernment so marked." "Between me and God," said Pwyll, "you ought rather to thank the man who was with you," and he told them what had happened. "Well, lord, thank God you made such a friend. As for the rule we have known this past year, surely you will not take it from us?" "Between me and God," said Pwyll, "I will not." From that time on the friendship between Pwyll and Arawn increased. Each sent the other horses and hounds and hawks and whatever treasure he thought his friend might like. Moreover, because of Pwyll's year-long sojourn in Annwvyn, because of his having reigned there so prosperously and his having united the two realms through valour and prowess, the name Pwyll, Lord of Dyved fell into disuse, and he was called Pwyll, Head of Annwvyn ever after.

—WALES, 14TH CENTURY

From *Manawydan Son of Llyr:*

In this selection, we see how a friendship develops between the principal characters of The Mabinogion: *Pwyll, Manawydan, and Rhiannon.*

After the seven men we mentioned above had buried Bran's head in the White Hill in London, with the face towards France, Manawydan looked at the town and at his friends, gave a great sigh and felt an immense sadness and longing. "Alas, almighty God, woe is reel" he said. "Among all those here I alone have no place for the night." "Lord, be not so heavy-hearted," said Pryderi. "Your cousin is king over the Island of the Mighty, and if he has wronged you, a still, you have never daimed land or property—you are one of the Three Ungrasping Chieftains." "Even though the king is my cousin," answered Manawydan, "it saddens me to see anyone in my brother Bran's place, and I could not be happy in the same house as Casswallawn." "Then will you listen to some more advice?" "I need advice. What is yours?" "The seven cantrevs of Dyved were left to me," said Pryderi, "and my mother Rhiannon is there. I will give her to you, along with authority over the seven cantrevs, and if you have no territory but these cantrevs, there are nonetheless no seven better than they. Kigva daughter of Gwynn the Splendid is my wife. Though the title to the land is mine, let it be you and Rhiannon who enjoy it, and should you ever desire territory perhaps you will have that too." "I do not desire that, chieftain," said Manawydan, "but God reward your friendship." "The truest friendship in my power shall be yours, if you want it." "I do want it, friend, and God reward you. I will go with you now to see Rhiannon and the territory." "That is the right thing to do," said Pryderi. "I do not imagine you have ever heard a lady talk better than she does; moreover when she was in her prime there was no lovelier woman, and even now her appearance will not disappoint you." They set out, and though their journey was long they finally reached Dyved, where Rhiannon and Kigva had prepared and set out a feast for them. Manawydan and Rhiannon sat together and began to talk; gradually his thoughts and desires grew tender towards her, and it pleased him that he had never seen a lovelier or more beautiful woman. "Pryderi, I will accept your offer," he said, whereupon Rhiannon asked, "What offer was that?" Pryderi answered. "Lady, I have given you as wife to Manawydan son of Llyr." "I accept that gladly," she said. "So do I," said Manawydan, "and God reward the man who gives me such true friendship." Before the feast ended, then, the couple slept together. "Continue with what remains of the feast," said Pryderi, "while I go to England to offer my submission to Casswallawn son of Beli" "Lord, Casswallawn is now in Kent," said Rhiannon. "You can continue with the feast and wait until he is nearer." "Then we will wait," said Pryderi. They continued the feast, and then they began a circuit of Dyved; they hunted and enjoyed themselves, and for roaming the countryside they had never seen a more delightful land, nor a better hunting-ground nor one better stocked with honey and fish. Such friendship arose among the four that none of them wished to be without the others day or night.

—WALES, 14TH CENTURY

Generosity

The ancient Celts considered generosity to be one of the three most important qualities that one could hope to possess. In all areas of life—personal relationships, legal matters, and matters of state—one's character was judged by his willingness to share his wealth or to come to the aid of a friend . . . or a stranger. The Brehon Laws of Ireland are based on this spirit of kindness and generosity, particularly the Law of Sick Maintenance, in which it was mandatory for an Irish citizen to care for a sick traveler. In *The Annals of Ulster*, men and women who were renowned for their generosity were the most celebrated, and in the bardic poems, kings are lauded for their kindness and hospitality. In this same way, the lack of a giving spirit can be the cause of ruin for a ruler.

It is also revealing that this spirit of kindness was not restricted to relationships between humans. One's courtesy towards animals was just as important as kindness towards one's fellow man, and such courtesy was often rewarded. This is especially apparent in *The Mabinogion* when Owein's generosity toward the lion ensures that the beast never leaves his side.

From *The Senchus Mor:*

Everyone receives the value of his qualifications according to his dignity both as to doctor's fees, company and food, and also in suitable cases, the compensation for maiming. All grades of the territory have the same right under the Law of Sick Maintenance.

—IRELAND, C. A.D. 438, FROM THE LAW OF SICK MAINTENANCE

From *the Senchus Mor:*

There is a stay also for providing him [the sick man] with proper bed furniture, i.e. plaids and bolsters, i.e. a suitable bed—for providing him with a proper house, i.e. that it be not a dirty snail-besmeared house, or that it be not one of the three inferior houses—i.e. that there be four doors out of it, in order that the sick man may be seen from every side, and water must run across the middle of it—for providing also against the things prohibited by the physician, i.e. that the sick man may not be injured, i.e. by women or dogs—i.e. that fools or female scolds be not let into the house to him, or that he be not injured by forbidden food. And he is a person whose death is not probable, and the stay is one day.

—IRELAND, C. A.D. 438, FROM THE LAW OF SICK MAINTENANCE

Healing

"Now Ireland both in extent of its breadth, wholesomeness and fineness of air, far passeth Britain. . . . Yea, more than that, all things in manner that cometh from said island is of sovereign virtue against poison. And this we saw with our own eyes, that when certain men that were stinged of venomous serpents had taken the scraped leaves of tree-stems which had been of Ireland . . . forthwith all the force of the spreading venom was utterly assuaged."

—THE VENERABLE BEDE, ON THE MAGICAL
CURING PROPERTIES OF IRELAND

In Celtic literature, the ability to heal another human being is portrayed as a divine gift. The power to heal a friend is considered even more precious. In the medieval Welsh poetry, the illness of a friend is heartbreaking to witness. In the Irish sagas, Oenghus would do everything in his power to heal his friend Cuchculainn.

Symbols of physical and spiritual healing are most often related to the restorative power of water in Celtic storytelling. In the Arthurian legends, the Holy Grail represents the healing of the soul and the promise of holiness. In the Welsh epic *The Mabinogion*, it is the cauldron that holds curative powers and promises spiritual regrowth.

The decision not to heal another human being is as revealing as the desire to cure. In *The Táin*, Cuchulainn is mortified to discover that he has inadvertently healed the Morrigan, the Irish goddess of war and death, and maintains that he would not have done so had her true identity been revealed to him.

In this selection from The Quest of the Holy Grail, *Sir Lancelot is healed by the power of God.*

On a day it befell, that in the Waste Forest, Galahad met Lancelot and Perceval, who did not know his shield. Lancelot was the first to make the attack, and broke his lance on Galahad's breast, but in return received such a stroke, that he went down, horse and man. After that, Galahad drew his sword, and fought with Perceval, whom he stunned with a blow that cleft cap and helm; the joust took place near a manor, where dwelt a recluse. When the latter saw Galahad, she said: "Sir knight, proceed under the guidance of God; had these knight known you as well as I, they would not have been so bold." When Galahad heard her, he feared to be discovered, and set off at speed; the others pursued as fast as they could, but were unable to overtake him. Lancelot and Perceval remained in the forest, and the latter wished to return by the road, but the former declared that he would follow the knight who carried the red shield.

Lancelot traversed the wood, but came to no path; he could find no refuge, for the night was dark. He kept on, until he arrived at a cross, and saw a stone with letters, which he could not make out. Near at hand, he perceived a chapel, and turned that way, hoping to find some inmate; at the entrance was an iron grating, that barred the passage; within, he saw an altar covered with a silken cloth, whereon stood a candlestick of seven branches, in which candles brightly burned. Vexed that he could not enter, he went back to his steed, and led him to the cross, removing saddle and bridle, that he might feed freely; Lancelot unlaced his helm, laid it beside him, and reclined beside the cross, but could not forget the good knight who carried the white shield.

At last, he saw approach a knight on a litter, borne on two palfreys; the knight groaned, as if in pain, and gazed on Lancelot, but said naught, for he thought him asleep; Lancelot never opened his lips, but lay between sleeping and waking. At the cross, the palfreys halted, and the knight exclaimed: "God have mercy, when will come the holy vessel, whereby shall be allayed the sharpness of this pain? Never for a fault hath any man suffered so much!" Thus, he lamented, bewailing his state; Lancelot looked, and saw the candlestick leave the chapel, and proceed to the cross, with no bearer; after the candles came to the Holy Grail, which he had seen in Camelot. When the sick man beheld this, he folded his hands and prayed: "Fair Lord God, who in this land by the power of thy holy vessel hast performed so many miracles, look favorably on me, that my pain be quelled, and that I may enter on the quest which the other lords have undertaken." With that, he dragged himself to the table whereon stood the vessel, and presses his lips to the stone on which it rested. Forthwith, he felt himself healed and cried: "Ha, God, I am cured!"

—FRANCE, C. A.D. 1140

In this selection from The Táin, *Cuchulainn inadvertently uses his power to heal the Morrigan, the goddess of death and war.*

Great weariness came over Cuchulainn after that night. The Morrigan appeared to him in the guise of an old hag engaged in milking a tawny, three-teated milch cow. Cuchulainn, maddened with thirst, begged her for a milking.

"May this be a cure in time for thee." Cuchulainn said. "The blessing of Gods and non-gods on you." And her head was healed and made whole. She gave him milk from second tit and her eyes were made whole thereby. She gave him milk from the third tit and her legs were made whole thereby.

"You said I should not get healing nor succor from thee forever," the Morrigan said.

"If I had known it was thou, I would never have healed thee,"
Cuchulainn made answer.

—IRELAND, 8TH CENTURY

From *The Wasting Sickness of Cuchulainn:*

In this selection from the saga The Wasting Sickness of
Cuchulainn, *Oenghus son of Aed Abrat vows to heal the great
warrior hero:*

Cuchulainn, sick as you are,
Waiting will be no help.
If they were yours, they would heal you,
The daughters of Aed Abrat.

Standing to the right of Labraid Luathlam,
In Mag Cruaich, Li Ban said
"Fand has expressed her desire
To lie down with Cuchulainn:

A joyous day it would be
Were Cuchulainn to come to my land.
He would have gold and silver
And plenty of wine to drink.

Were he my friend now,
Cuchulainn son of Sualtaim,
Perhaps he could relate what he saw
In his sleep, apart from the host.

There at Mag Muirthemni in the south
No misfortune will befall you in this Samuin."
I will send Li Ban to you,
Cuchulainn, sick as you are.

—IRELAND, 8TH CENTURY

The following is a healing poem by Guto'r Glyn, the great me-
dieval Welsh poet (c. 1420–1493), who vows to go to any lengths
to heal a sick friend.

A HEALING CYWYDD,
for Hywel of Moelyrch
Hywel ab Ieuan Fychan, I won't sleep much
(a gray-white stag) because you're not well.
My lot is anxiety
if you're sick.
If you're healed (God can do it)
from your wound, I'm fine and very fit.
If you're sick, my Mordaf,
sick, weak do I feel myself too.
Your sad fall takes me out of my good state,
your joint brings me affliction.
Bitter and costly to the commons
of your land was the wounding of your knee.

All the world was threatened (yours is a beautiful nature)
because of your knee pain.
I wept in Moelyrch,
the size of the fall, a troop seek him out.
The wandering poets were sad for your great wound;
I'm still sad for you.

A pity is the bandage on a generous man;
we mourn that a stingy man didn't get it
By the true God, I'd laugh
if it were on some of those I know!
Hippocrates (a noble David)
will pull you free of the bandage.
A Mary Magdalene is modest Elen,

she cares for you, a long task.
The salve of the woman who was Jesus' physician
made a dear remedy,
and with her salve.
May beautiful Elen's efforts do the same for your knee.
One who'd love eaves and the fresh woods
and God's grace and the day's warmth
and the virtue of summer's nature
will break the pangs of winter.
The sound of the poetry of our kinsman Taliesin
got his master out of prison.
I have a mind, because of what I might compose,
to get the knee out of the prison of a wound.
Many a person (you're gold handed)
was healed with a Cywydd.
I swear by the fire, I too
will make an ointment of praise for you.
And if the mouth (and what it made)
doesn't have the power of a medication,
the host of heaven will make you merrily well.
Behold! Everybody's merrier!
Generous Saint Silin (better than the chill of an ointment)
blesses you:
Oswald, the fine haired king,
will rid the knee of the leg wound;
Mary, with your gold and myrrh and incense;
may Martin be assisting!
Gwenfrewy will full overcome complaint and disease,
injury and wound.
The miracles of Ieuan of Gwanas
will drive it from the knee, with the silver cross.
Curig will be your physician;
Christ himself, of execution's cross.

With Saint Lednart, our kinsman, we'll get
to fetch you out of prison.
Go to Melangell now,
arise, O Nudd, you'll get to be well.
I won't sing bold praise poetry.
I won't laugh until you walk.

—WALES, 15TH CENTURY

Honor

There is perhaps no more valued tenet in the Celtic moral code than honor. A Celtic warrior had no reservations about fighting to the death to defend another's honor, and more importantly the honor of his family and his name. For the Celtic hero, preserving his honor was more important than preserving his life. Honor is an especially key theme in *The Táin*, where it is the prime motivation for most of the characters' actions. The decision to sleep with someone, kill someone, or engage in battle is almost solely based on maintaining one's own honor, the honor of one's country, or the honor of a lover. In de Troyes' *The Search of the Holy Grail*, King Arthur implores Gawain to help him restore his honor, his most precious possession. It is this deep admiration for the concept of honor and chivalry that would continue to influence medieval literature throughout Europe.

From *Cuchulainn's Courtship of Emer:*

The king accompanied Forgall to his fort for the wedding. Emer was brought to Lugaid's place to sit by his side, but she held both her hands to his cheeks and swore on his life and his honour that it was Cuchulainn she loved, and that for any one else to take her as his wife would be suffer loss of honour. Lugaid didn't dare sleep with Emer then for fear of Cuchulainn, and he turned home again.

— IRELAND, 8TH CENTURY

119

From *Rochad's Bloodless Fight, The Táin:*

Cuchulain dispatched his charioteer to Rochad Rigderg (Red-king) son of Fathemon from Rigdorn in the north that he should come to his aid. He was of Ulster. The gilla comes up to Rochad and tells him, if he has come out of his weakness, to go to the help of Cuchulainn, that they should employ a ruse to reach the host to seize some of them and slay them. Rochad set out from the north. Thrice fifty warriors was his number, and he took posession of a hill fronting the hosts. "Scan the plain for us today," said Ailill. " I see a company crossing the plain," the watchman answered, "and a tender youth comes in their midst; the other warriors each but up his shoul-der." "Who is that warrior, O Fergus?" asked Ailill. "Rochad son of Fathemon," he answered; "and it is to bring help to Cuchulain he comes." "I know what ye had best do with him," Fergus continued. "Let a hundred warriors go from ye with the maiden yonder to the middle of the plain and let the maid go before them, and let a horse-man go tell Rochad to come alone to hold converse with the maid and let hands be laid on him, and thus shall be removed all fear of his people from us." Finnabair, daughter of Ailill and Medb, perceived that and she went to speak to her mother thereof, even yo Medb. Now it happened that Finnabair loved Rochad. It is he was the fairest young warrior in Ulster at that time. And Finnabair disclosed her secret and her love to her mother. "Truly have I loved yonder warrior for a long time," said she: "and it is he is my sweetheart, my first love and mine own choice one in wooing of the men of Erin." "And thou hast so loved him daughter," quoth Ailill and Medb, "sleep with him this night and crave for us a truce of him for the hosts, until with Conchobar he encounters us on the day of the great battle when four of the grand provinces of Erin will meet at Garech and Ilgarech in the battle of the Foray of Cualnge."

This then is done. Rochad sets forth to meet the horseman. "I am come," says the horseman, "from Finnabair to meet thee

that thou come speak with the maiden." Thereupon Rochad
goes alone to converse with her. The army surrounds him on all
sides; he is seized and hands are laid on him; his followers are
routed and driven in flight. Afterwards he is set free and bound
over to not to oppose Ailill's host till the time he will come
with all the warriors of Ulster. After they promise to give
Finnabair to him Rochad son of Fathemon accepted the offer
and there-upon he left them and that night the damsel slept
with him.

An Under-king of Munster that was in the camp heard the
tale. He went to his people to speak of it. "Yonder maiden was
plighted to me on fifteenhostages once long ago," said he; "and it
is for this I have now come on this hosting." Now wherever it
happened that the seven Under-kings of Munster were, what they
all said was for this they were come. "Yonder maiden was pledged
to each of us in the bargain as our sole wife, to the end that we
should take part in this warfare." They all declared that this was
the price and condition on which they had come on the hosting.
"Why," said they, "What better counsel could we take? Should we
not go to avenge our wife and our honour on the Mane' the sons
of Ailill who are watching and guarding the rear of the army at
Imlech in Glendamrach?"

This was the course they resolved upon. And with their
seven divisions of thirty hundreds they arose each man of them to
attack the Mane'. When Ailill heard that, he arose with a start
with ready shield against them and thirty hundred after them.
Medb arose with her thirty hundred. The sons of Maga with
theirs and the Leinsterman and the Mustermen and the people of
Tara.

Then arose Fergus with his thirty hundred to intervene between them, and that was a hand for that mighty work. And a
mediation was made between them so that each of them sat down
near the other and hard by his arms. Howbeit before the interven-

tion took place, eight hundred, very valiant warriors of them had fallen in the slaughter of Glenn Domain.

Finnabair, daughter of Ailill and Medb, had tidings that so great a number of the men of Erin had fallen for her sake and on account of her. And her heart broke in her breast even as a nut, through shame and disgrace, so that Finnabair Slebe (Finnabair of the Mount) is the name of the place where she fell, died, and was buried.

—IRELAND, 8TH CENTURY

From *Arthur—The Quest of the Holy Grail:*

In this selection from The Hunt of The White Stag *by Chrétien de Troyes, we see just how important the code of honor was in the court of King Arthur. Here Queen Guinevere has been humiliated by a dwarf and her husband must find a way to avenge her, without losing face himself:*

Queen Guinevere with Erec and the damsel, halted and listened; but the hunt was so far away they could make out neither horn nor hound. They halted in a clearing by the side of the track; and it was not long before they saw approaching a knight on a charger, fully armed, beside whom rode a fair maiden, while in front went a crooked dwarf, bearing a knotted scourge. The queen admired the knight, and wondered who he could be. "Girl," she said, "bid yonder knight come, and bring his damsel." The maid ambled; but the cross dwarf met her, scourge in hand. "Stop, damsel! What seek you? You must go no farther." "Dwarf, let me pass! I must speak with yonder knight, for the queen hath sent me." The peevish dwarf blocked her road: "Here you have no errand! Back! You are not fit to accost so good a knight." The girl would have forced her way, for she scorned the dwarf, seeing how little he was; but when he saw her approach, he raised his thong and smote her on the back of the hand, so that it left a red mark.

Lief or loath, the damsel could do no more; she returned, tears coursing down her cheeks. When the queen perceived her maiden hurt, she was at a loss: "Ha, Erec, fair friend, I am sorry for my girl, whom this wicked dwarf hath beaten; churlish is the knight, to let such a monster harm a creature so fair. Sweet friend, go, bid him come hither, fail not; I wish to know him, himself, and his friend." Erec spurred; but when he saw him draw near, the dwarf went to meet him: "Vassal, stand back! Here I know not your errand!" "Begone, tiresome dwarf! You are too cross and contrary! Let me pass!" "You shall not!" "I will!" "You shall not!" With that, Erec thrust aside the dwarf; but he, who was fell, raised his thong and smote Erec on the neck, and in the face, so that the welt showed from cheek to cheek. Erec knew that by blows there was naught to be gained, for he saw that the armed knight was rude and feared to be slain if before his eyes he beat his dwarf; rashness is not courage. He returned and said: "Lady, now 'tis worse; this bad dwarf hath spoiled my face. I dared not touch him, but none hath right to blame me, for arms had I none, and I dreaded the knight, who is churlish and outrageous; he would not jest but kill me in his pride. I promise you, if I can, I will avenge my shame, or increase it; my arms will not avail me, I shall not get them against my need; this morn, when I came away, I left them at Cardigan; if I went to seek them, I should never overtake the knight, for he rideth fast. I must follow him, far or near, until I find a man of whom I can hire arms or who will lend them to me. If I get them, then the knight will find me ready to do battle; be assured, we shall fight until he master me, or I him. If I can, I will arrive on the third day; you will see me at the castle, glad or grieved. Lady, I may tarry no longer; I commend you to God." The queen, on her part, a hundred times bade him be in the keeping of God, with prayers that he might be delivered from harm.

Erec departed, and the queen remained in the forest, where the king had overtaken the stag, for no other was in at the death.

They returned to Cardigan, bearing the venison; and after supper, when the barons were merry in hall, the king declared, that since he had captured the stag he would take the kiss, to make good the custom. Then rose a murmur, while every knight said to his neighbour, that it would not pass without controversy of sword or ashen lance, for each was prepared to prove, by dint of blows, that his own friend was fairest in the hall. When Sir Gawain heard, be sure he was vexed; he took the king to speech, and said: "Sir, in dismay are your knights; all speak of this kiss, and affirm that it will not be given without quarrel and strife." Of his wisdom, the king returned: "Fair nephew, counsel me, save my honor and right, for uproar I would not have."

To counsel ran the best barons, King Ider first, and after him King Cadwallon, wise and brave, with Kei and Girflet, King Amangon, and other barons enow. The debate lasted until the queen appeared, and recited the adventure of the armed knight, whom she had met in the wood, and the felon dwarf, that had scourged the girl and struck Erec, who had gone after to avenge his shame: and she cried: "Sir, delay a little, for my sake! If these barons agree, defer the kiss until the third day, when Erec will arrive." All gave consent, and the king acceded to her suit.

—FRANCE, C. A.D. 1140

From *The Bruce:*

The Bruce *remains one of the great epic poems of medieval liter-ature. Written by John Barbour in the fourteenth century, it is an ode to the bravery and principle of Robert the Bruce, the renowned Scottish hero who refused to serve as vassal under the English king, King Edward I, and who fought for his right to rule an in-dependent Scotland. In the following verses, Sir Robert defies Edward, clearly aware that the king is trying to deceive him, by asserting that he will rule Scotland on his own terms. By stand-*

*ing his ground, he thereby retains his honor. In contrast, we see
that John of Baliol accepts Edward's invitation to be a nominal
king, thereby losing his own.*

When Edward heard how matters lay
He changed his plans without delay;
Forthwith abandoned his crusade
And back to England journey made.
And soon to Scotland word he sent
That they should hold a parliament,
And that he would hasten there to do
In all things they asked him to do.
He reckoned by their differences,
That he would soon make all things his,
And find some method underhand
By which to occupy their land!

And then to Robert the Bruce said he:
"If thou wilt govern under me
For evermore, and thine offspring,
I will decide that thou be king."

"Sir," said the Bruce, "so God me save!
The kingdom little do I crave.
But if it falls right of me,
And if God wills so that it be.
Then I shall reign in everything
As freely as behooves a king;
Or as my forebears formerly
Have reigned, in fullest royalty!"

The other rose in rage, and swore
That he should have if never more.

And turned himself with wrath away.
But John of Baliol that day
Assented to his terms in all;
Whereof did greatest ill befall.
For he was king but little while,
And through great subtlety and guile,
For little reason or for none
Was soon arrested and undone.
And presently bereft was he
Of honour and of dignity.
Whether it was of wrong or right
God knows, that is the God of Might!

In this way dealt that mighty king
Sir Edward to his own liking
With John of Baliol, that so soon
Was overthrown and brought to ruin.

—SCOTLAND, 14TH CENTURY

Knowledge

"It is said that during their training they learn by heart a great many verses, so that many people spend twenty years studying the doctrine. They do not think it right to commit their teachings to writing, although for almost all other purposes, for example, for public and private accounts, they use the Greek alphabet. . . . They did not want their doctrines to be accessible to the ordinary people, and they did not want their pupils to rely on the written word and so neglect to train their memories. For it does usually happen that if people have the help of written documents, they do not pay as much attention to learning by heart, and so let their memories become less efficient."

—Julius Caesar, on the unique method of imparting knowledge
used by the Druids, the Celts' religious leaders

In ancient Ireland, religious leaders called Druids were so revered for their knowledge and wisdom that they were thought to possess extraordinary powers. Even the fiercest warrior bowed in the presence of these great men of learning, as Diodorous Siculus observed:

And it is not only in the needs of peace but also in war that they carefully obey these men and their song-loving poets, and this is true not only of their friends but of their enemies. For oft-times as armies approached each

127

other in the line of battle with their swords drawn and their spears raised for the charge, these men come forth between them and stop the conflict as they had spellbound some kind of wild animals. Thus, even among the most savage barbarians, anger yields to wisdom, and Ares does homage to the muse.

In ancient Irish societies, it was the poets and priests (along with the chieftains) who made up the "saer" or noble class, and those who possessed verbal skill and good judgment were celebrated above all. The Brehon Laws make special provisions for citizens who possessed literary skill, and deem learned and skilled men and women to be the highest class of person. As Peter Beresford observes in *The Celtic Empire*, "to the Celts, the soul was contained in the head and not in the heart," which may explain the Celtic fascination with all matters concerning the head—including intellect and knowledge.

In Irish mythology, Druids and poets are celebrated for their unique knowledge, particularly in the stories in the *Book of Invasions* and the Ulster and the *Ossian Cycles*.

From *The Conquest of the Tuatha Dé Danann:*

In ancient Ireland, The Book of Invasions *was a collection of stories that served to reflect the history of Ireland's people. In the tale* The Conquest of the Tuatha Dé Danann, *we are introduced to the Tuatha Dé, great men of learning who were thought to possess extraordinary powers because of their superior knowledge.*

As for Iobath son of Beothach son of Iarbanel son of Nemed, after his leaving Ireland with his people after the conquest before described, they settled in the northern islands of Greece. They were there till numerous were their children and their kindred.

They learned druidry and many various arts in the islands where they were, what with *fithnaisecht, amaitecht, conbliocht,* and every sort of gentilism in general, until they were knowing, learned, and very accomplished in the branches thereof. They were called Tuatha Dé; that is, they considered their men of learning to be gods, and their husbandmen non-gods, so much was their power in every art and every druidic occultism besides. Thence came the name, which is Tuatha Dé, to them.

—IRELAND, FIRST WRITTEN DOWN C. 8TH CENTURY

From *The Mabinogion:*

In this selection, Arthur shows his reverence for Cadyryeith son of Seidi, a young man who is wise beyond his years, and who, because of his immense knowledge, gains pride of place in Arthur's court:

"Iddawg, who is that auburn-haired man to whom they have come?" asked Rhonabwy. "Rhun son of Maelgwn of Gwynedd, a man whose status is such that everyone comes to him for advice." "And why was a lad as young as Cadyryeith son of Seidi brought into the council of such high-ranking men?" "Because no one in Britain gives better advice." At that Arthur's bards began to chant a song, which no man there except Cadyryeith himself understood, except that it was in praise of Arthur. Then twenty-four donkeys came with baskets of gold and silver, and with each donkey a tired exhausted man bringing Arthur tribute from the islands of Greece. Cadyryeith son of Seidi asked that Osla Big Knife be granted a truce to the end of a month and a fortnight, and that the donkeys which brought the tribute be given to the Bards, along with the baskets, as a reward for their patience, and that during the truce they be rewarded for their songs, and all this was agreed upon. "Rhonabwy," said Iddawg, "would it not be wrong to prevent a young man who gives such abundant advice from attending his lord's council?" Then Kei rose and said, "Whoever wishes to follow Arthur, let him be in Cornwall tonight, and let everyone else come to meet Arthur at the end of the truce."

—WALES, 14TH CENTURY

From *The Boyhood Deeds of Finn:*

In this selection from The Cycle of Finn, *we are first introduced to Finn, the great Irish hero who is fated to eat from the coveted Salmon of Fec, and therefore gains infinite wisdom. Throughout Celtic literature, the salmon remains a magical animal who possesses great knowledge. In this passage, the salmon imparts the greatest gifts of all—the ability to craft poetry.*

Thereupon Finn went into Connacht, and found Crimall as an old man in a desert wood there, and a number of the old fian together with him; and it is they who did the hunting for him. Then he showed the bag and told his story from the beginning to end; how he had slain the man of the treasures. Finn bade farewell to Crimall, and went to learn poetry from Finneces, who was on the Boyne. He durst not remain in Ireland else, until he took to poetry, for fear of the sons of Urgriu, and of the sons of Morna.

Seven years Finneces had been on the Boyne, watching the Salmon of Fec's pool; for it had been prophesied of him that he would eat the Salmon of Fec, after which nothing would be unknown to him. The salmon was found, and Demne was ordered to cook it; and the poet told him not to eat anything of the salmon. The youth brought him the salmon after cooking it. "Hast thou eaten any of the salmon, my lad?" said the poet.

"No," said the youth, "but I burned my thumb, and put into my mouth afterwards."

"What is thy name, my lad?" said he.

"Demne," said the youth.

"Finn is thy name, my lad," said he, "and to thee was the salmon given to be eaten, and indeed thou art the Finn." Thereupon the youth ate the salmon. It is that which gave the knowledge to Finn, so that, whenever he put his thumb into his mouth and sang through teinm laida, then whatever he had been ignorant of would be revealed to him.

He learnt the three things that constitute a poet: *teinm laida* (a magic formula), *imbas forosna* (illuminating inspiration), and *dichetul dichennaib* (magic gifts).

—IRELAND, C. 8TH CENTURY

Love

Like all themes in Celtic literature, love in its various forms is always portrayed as unbridled and unbidden. Love between friends is just as passionate as love between men and women. This is particularly true in *The Táin*, in which same-sex friendships between men are all-encompassing. The love between Ferdiad and Cuchulainn is just as powerful as the love that Cuchulainn shares with his wife, Emer. In the later Welsh and Scottish literature, the concept of love becomes more romantic, but no less passionate. In *The Mabinogion*, the man or woman who falls in love will risk everything to please the objection of his or her passion—including death.

From *The Two Lovers*, an ancient Breton tale:

In this beautiful Breton story, a young couple's love is so passionate that it eventually kills them, but because their love was so strong, they become part of the landscape.

In Normandy, of old, there fell an adventure oft recounted; t'is a tale of two children who loved one another, and how both through their love died. Of this the Bretons made a lay and called it "Les Dous Amanz."

Know ye that in Neustria, which we call Normandy, it is a great mountain marvelous high, and on its summit lie the two lovers. Near to this mountain on one side, a king with great care and counsel built him a city; lord he was of the Pistreis, and because of his folk, he called the town Pitres. Still has the name endured, and there to this day may ye see houses and city; and all that region, as is well known, men called the Vale of Pitres. This king had a daughter, a fair damsel and a courteous; no other child had he and much he loved and cherished her. She was sought for in marriage by many a great lord, who would gladly have taken her to wife; but the king would give her to none, for that he could not bear to part with her. No other companion had he, but kept her with him night and day, for since the death of the queen she was his only solace. Yet many a one held it ill done on his part, and even his own household blamed him for it. And when he knew that men talked thereof, much it grieved and troubled him; and he began to bethink him how he might so contrive that none would willingly seek his daughter. And then he let it be known far and wide, that whosoever would have the maiden, must know one thing of a sooth; it was decreed and appointed that her suitor should carry her in his arms, with no stop for rest upon the way, to the summit of the mountain without the city. When the news thereof were made known and spread abroad through the land, many a one assayed the feat but none might achieve it. Some there were who with much striving carried her mid-way up the mountain; then they could go no farther but must needs let be. So for a long space the damsel remained unwedded and no man would ask her in marriage.

In the same land was a damoiseau, son to a count he was, and full and fresh and fair; and much he strove in well doing that he might have praise above all others. He frequented the kings court and often sojourned there; and he grew to love the king's daughter, and ofttimes besought her that she would grant him her favour, and love him with all her love. And in that he was brave and courteous, and much praised of the king, she granted him her grace, and in all humility he rendered her thanks therefor. Often they held speech together, and loyally each loved the other, yet they concealed it the best they might, that none should know therof. Grievous was this time to them, but the youth bethought him that it was better to endure this evil than to make haste over much only to fail; yet was he brought to sore anguish through love. And it fell on a time that the damoiseau who so fait and valiant came unto his love, and speaking, made her his plait. Piteously he besought her that she should flee thence with him, for he could no longer endure his pain; yet he knew full well that were he to ask her of her father, he loved her so much he would give her to none who did not first bear her in his arms to the top of the mountain. Then the damsel made answer: "Dear heart, I know full well you could not carry me so far, for your strength is not great enough; yet were I to flee with you my father would suffer so great dolour and grief it were torment for him to live; and of a sooth I hold him so dear and love him so much I would not willingly bring him sorrow.

—FRANCE, C. 12TH CENTURY

In this later version of the Cuchulainn and Emer love story, The Courting of Emer, *the Irish hero first sees the woman who will become his wife and his great love.*

When Cuchulainn was growing out of his boyhood at Emain Macha, all the women of Ulster loved him for his skill in feats, for the lightness of his leap, for the weight of his wisdom, for the sweetness of his speech, for the beauty of his face, for the loveliness of his looks, for all his gifts. He had the gift of caution in fighting, until such time as his anger would come on him, and the hero light would shine about his head; the gift of feats, the gift of chess-playing, the gift of draught-playing, the gift of counting, the gift of divining, the gift of right judgment, the gift of beauty. And all the faults they could find in him were three, that he was too young and smooth-faced, so that young men who did not know him would be laughing at him, that he was too daring, and that he was too beautiful.

The men of Ulster took counsel together then about Cuchulainn, for their women and their maidens loved him greatly, and it is what they settled among themselves, that they would seek out a young girl that would be a fitting wife for him, the way that their own wives and their daughters would not be making so much of him. And besides that they were afraid he might die young, and leave no heir after him.

So Conchobar set out nine men into each of the provinces of Ireland to look for a wife for Cuchulainn, to see if in any dun or in any chief place, they could find the daughter of a king or of an owner of a land or a householder, who would be pleasing to him, that he might ask her in marriage.

All of the messengers came back at the end of a year, but not one of them had found a young girl that would please Cuchulainn. And then he himself went out to court a young girl he knew in Luglochta Loga, the Garden of Lugh, Emer, the daughter of Forgall Manach, the Wily.

He set in his chariots, that all the chariots of Ulster could not follow by reason of its swiftness, and of the chariot chief who sat in it. And he found the young girl on her playing field, with her companions about her, daughters of the landowners that lived near Forgall's dun, and they learning needlework and fine embroidery from Emer. And of all the young girls of Ireland, she was the one Cuchulainn thought worth courting; for she had the six gifts—the gift of beauty, the gift of voice, the gift of sweet speech, the gift of needlework, the gift of wisdom, the gift of chastity. And Cuchulainn had said that no woman should marry him but one that was his equal in age, in appearance, and in race, in skill and handiness; and one who was the best worker with her needle of the young girls of Ireland, for that would be the only one would be a fitting wife for him. And that is why it was Emer he went to ask above all others.

—IRELAND, 8TH CENTURY

From *The Exile of the Sons of Usnech:*

The story of Deirdre, which appears in The Exile of the Sons of Usnech, *is one of the most famous—and most tragic—love stories in the Irish* Ulster Cycle. *In this tale, the beautiful but cursed heroine is destined from birth to bring woe to all who enter her life, including her lover and his family. In this selection, Deirdre first sees the handsome Naisi, for whom she will later jeopardize her loveless marriage to the elderly King Conchobar. Here we see that Deirdre's passion and willingness to sacrifice everything for love is all-consuming, and will later have dire consequences.*

Now it chanced upon a certain day in the time of winter that the foster-mother of Deirdre was outside the house, skinning a calf upon the snow, in order to cook it for her, and the blood of the calf lay upon the snow, and she saw a black raven which came down to drink it. "Leborcham," said Deirdre, "that man only will I love, who hath the three colors that I see yonder—his hair as black as the raven, his cheeks red like the blood, and his body as white as the snow."

"Blessing and good fortune to thee!" said Leborcham, "That man is not far away. He is yonder in the stronghold of Emain Macha, which is nigh; and the name of him is Naisi, the son of Usnech."

"I shall never be in good health again," said Deirdre, "until the time comes when I may see him."

—IRELAND, 8TH CENTURY

From *The Wooing of Étain:*

In The Wooing of Étain, *the beautiful medieval Irish love story, Eochaid Airem, the ancient high king of Ireland, pursues*

*the lovely maiden Étain and seeks to make her his wife. In this se-
lection, Étain first meets the king, and declares that she has always loved him for his inner beauty and nobility, even before
setting eyes on him.*

A desire for her seized the king immediately, and he sent a
man of his company to hold her before him. Then Eochaid approached the maiden and questioned her. "Whence art thou, O
maiden?" said the king, "and whence hast thou come?"

"Not hard to answer," replied the maiden. "Étain the daughter of the king of Echrad out of the fairy-mounds I am called."

"Shall I have an hour of dalliance with thee?" said Eochaid.

"It is for that I have come hither under thy protection," said
she. "I have been here for twenty years since I was born in the
fairy-mound, and the men of the fairy-mound, both kings and
nobles, have been wooing me, and naught was got by any of them
from me, because I have loved thee and given love and affection to
thee since I was a little child and since I was capable of speaking.
It was for the noble tales about thee and for thy splendour that I
have loved thee, and, although I have never seen thee before, I
recognized thee at once by thy description. It is thou, I know, to
whom I have attained," said she.

"That is by no means the invitation of a bad friend," replied
Eochaid; "thou shalt be welcomed by me, and all other women
shall be left for thy sake, and with thee alone will I live as long as
it is pleasing to thee."

—IRELAND, 8TH CENTURY

From *The Dean Of Lismore:*
We see affection and love beautifully depicted in this poem from
The Dean of Lismore, *in which a warrior dies to fulfill the
wishes of his beloved.*

'Tis the sigh of a friend from Fraoch's green mound,
'Tis the warrior's sigh from his lonely bier,
'Tis a sigh might grieve the manly heart,
And might make a maid to weep.
Here to the east the cairn, where lies
Fraoch Fithich's son of softest locks,
Who nobly strove to favor Mai,
And from whom Cairn Fraoch is named.
In Cruachan east a woman weeps,
In mournful tale 'tis she laments;
Heavy, heavy sigh she gives
For Fraoch mac Fithich of ancient fame.
She 'tis, in truth, who sorely weeps,
As Fraoch's green mound she visits oft;
Maid of the locks that wave so fair,
Mai's daughter, so beloved of men.
This night Orla's soft-haired daughter,
Lies side by side with Fraoch mac Fithich.
Many were the men who loved her,
She, of them all, loved Fraoch alone.
His body got its grevious wounds,
Because with her he'd do no wrong;
She doomed him to a bitter death:
Judge not of women by her deed,
Grief 'twas that he should fall by Mai,
Yet I'll relate it without guile. A sigh.

A rowan tree stood in Loch Mai,
We see its shore there to the south;
Every quarter every month,
It bore its fair, well-ripened fruit;
There stood the tree alone, erect,

Its fruit than honey sweeter far;
That precious fruit so richly red,
Did suffice for a man's nine meals;
A year it added to man's life,—
The tale I tell is very truth.
Health to the wounded it could bring.
Such virtue had its red-skinned fruit.
One thing alone was to be feared
By him who sought men's ills to soothe:
A monster fierce lay at its root,
Which they who sought its fruit must fight.
A heavy, heavy sickness fell
On Athach's daughter, of liberal horn;
Her messenger she sent for Fraoch,
Who asked her what 'twas ailed her now.
Mai said her health would never return,
Unless her fair soft palm was filled
With berries from the deep cold lake,
Gleaned by the hand of none but Fraoch.
"Ne'er have I yet request refused,"
Said Fithich's son of ruddy hue;
"Whate'er the lot of Fraoch may be,
The berries I will pull for Mai."
The fair-formed Fraoch then moved away
Down to the lake, prepared to swim.
He found the monster in deep sleep,
With head up-pointed to the tree. A sigh.

Fraoch Fithich's son of pointed arms,
Unheard by the monster, then approached.
He plucked a bunch of red-skinned fruit,
And brought it to where Mai did lie.

"Though what thou did'st thou hast done well,"
Said Mai, she of form so fair,
"My purpose nought, brave man, wilt serve,
But that from the root thoud'st tear the tree."
No bolder heart there was than Fraoch's,
Again the slimy lake he swam;
Yet great as was his strength, he couldn't
Escape the death for him ordained.
Firm by the top he seized the tree,
And from the root did tear it up;
With speed again he makes for land,
But not before the beast awakes.
Fast he pursues, and, as he swam,
Seized in his horried maw his arm.
Fraoch by the jaw then grasped the brute,
'Twas sad for him to want his knife:
The maid of softest waving hair,
In haste brought him a knife of gold.
The monster tore his soft white skin,
And hacked most grievously his arm.
Then they fell, sole to sole opposed,
Down to the southern stony strand.
Fraoch mac Fithich, he and the beast,
'Twere well that they had never fought.
Fierce was the conflict, yet 'twas long,—

The monster's head at length he took.
When the maid what happened saw,
Upon the strand she fainting fell.
Then from her trance when she awoke,
In her soft hand she seized his hand:
"Although for wild birds thou art food,

Thy last exploit was nobly done."
'Tis from that death which he met then,
The name is given to Loch Mai;
That name it will forever bear,
Men have called it so till now. A sigh.

—SCOTLAND, C. 16TH CENTURY

Love of Nature

In the Celtic world, the absolute respect for animals and nature influenced law, religion, and poetry. In Irish society, animals had rights under the Brehon Laws, and were protected by their own deity, Cernunnos, a nature god who lorded over beasts of the forest and the natural world. In Welsh poetry, the power and holiness of nature is particularly exalted in the hermit and gnomic poems. Similarly, the Irish poems of the twelfth-century saint Colum Cille reflect the Celtic belief that to show respect for nature is to show respect for God.

In this transporting poem from the medieval Irish saint Colum Cille, he conveys his belief that appreciation of nature is its own form of prayer.

Delightful I think it to be in the bosom of an isle
On the crest of a rock,
That I may look there on the manifold
Face of the sea.

That I may see its heavy waves
Over the glittering ocean
As they chant a melody to their Father
On their eternal course.

That I may see its smooth strand of clear headlands,
No gloomy thing;

That I may hear the voice of the wondrous birds,
A wondrous course.

That I may hear the sound of the shallow waves
Against the rocks;
That I may hear the cry beside the churchyard,
The roar of the sea.

That I may see its splendid flock of birds
Over the full-watered ocean;
That I may see its mighty whales, greatest
Of wonders.

That I may see its ebb and flood-tide
In its flow;
That this should be my name, a secret I declare,
"He who turned his back on Ireland."

That contrition of heart should come upon me
When I look on it;
That I may bewail my many sins
Difficult to declare.

That I may bless the Lord
Who has power over all,
Heaven with its crystal order of angels,
Earth, ebb, flood-tide.

That I may pore on one of my books,
Good for my soul,
A while kneeling for beloved heaven,
A while at psalms.

A while meditating upon the Prince of Heaven,
Holy is the redemption,
A while at labour not too heavy;
It would be delighful!

A while gathering dilisk from the rock,
A while fishing,
A while giving food to the poor,
A while in my cell.

The counsel which is best before God
Me may confirm it to me,
May the King, whose servant I am, not desert me.
May he not deceive me.

—IRELAND, EARLY 12TH CENTURY

Here, the poet Oisin conveys the beauty of the hill Benn Boilbin to St. Patrick.

Benn Boilbin that is sad to-day,
Peak that was shapely and best of form,
At that time, son of Calpurnius,
It was lovely to be upon its crest.

Many were the dogs and the ghillies,
The cry of the bugle and the hound,
And the mighty heroes that were upon your rampart,
Oh high peak of the contest.

It was haunted by cranes in the night,
And heath fowl on its moors,
With the tuning of small birds.
It was delightful to be listening to them.

The cry of the hounds in its glens,
The wonderful echo,
And each of the Fiana
With lovely dogs on the leash.

Many in the wood were the gleaners
From the fair women of the Fiana,
Its berries of sweet taste,
Raspberries and blackberries.

Mellow purple blaeberries,
Tender cress and cuckoo-flower;
And the curly-haired fair-headed maids,
Sweet was the sound of their singing.

It was cause to be joyous
To be looking and listening
To the lonesome scream of the eagle,
To the murmur of the otters and the talk of the foxes.

The blackbird at Inbher Scieche
Singing most sweetly,
I swear to you, Patrick.
It was a delightful place.

We were on this hill seven companies of the Fiana;
To-night my friends are few,
And is not my tale pitiful to you?

—IRELAND, C. 5TH CENTURY

From the *Four Old Irish Songs of Summer and Winter:*

*In this selection, Finn comforts his servant with the glorious im-
ages of summer when he complains about inclement weather.*

Summer has come, healthy and free.
At which the dark wood becomes bowed;
At the slender nimble dear leaps
When the path of seals is smooth.

The cuckoo sings sweet soft music
At which there is tranquil unbroken sleep,
Gentle birds hop about the knoll
And swift gray stags.

Heat has laid hold on the repose of the deer,
Pleasant is the cry of active packs;
The white stretch of the strand smiles
Where the brisk sea is turbulent.

The noise of wanton winds in the top
Of the dark oakwood of Drum Daill;
The noble hornless herd runs
To which Cuan Wood is a shelter.

Green bursts out on every plant,
Wooded is the copse of the green oak-grove;
Summer has come, winter has gone,
Tangled hollies wound the hound.

The hardy blackbird sings a strain,
To whom the thorny wood is a heritage;
The sad turbulent sea is sleeping,
The speckled salmon leaps.

The sun smiles on every land,
I am free from the brood of
Hounds bark, stags assemble,
Ravens flourish, Summer has come.

In this selection, the Welsh gnomic poet shows his respect for the power of nature to turn brutal.

Winter's Day, hard are the berries,
Leaves aloft, the pond is full;
The morning before his going
Woe to him who trusts a stranger.

Winter's Day; fine is a secret shared;
The wind is as swift as a storm;
It is the work of a skillful man to hide a secret.

Winter's Day, thin are the stags,
Yellow are the tops of the birches,
The summer steading is deserted;
Woe to him who incurs shame for a trifle.

Winter's Day, bent are the tops of the branches;
Usual is commotion from the mouth of the mischievous;
Where there is no natural gift there will be no learning.

Winter's Day, rough is the weather, unlike early summer;
There is no diviner but God.

Winter's Day; sweet-songed are the birds;
Short is the day; loud are cuckoos;
The merciful providence of God is best.

Winter's Day; what is parched is hard;
Very black is the raven, swift is the sturdy;
The youth laughs when the old man stumbles.

Winter's Day, thin are the stags;
Woe to the weak when he is angry; ephemeral will be
The world, better is kindness than comeliness.

Winter's Day, bare is the burning, the plough is in the fur-
row, the ox at work;
From a hundred scarcely a friend.

—FROM THE WELSH GNOMIC POETS, EARLY 12TH CENTURY

From *The Birchtree:*

*In this poem, the great medieval poet Dafydd Llwyd pays homage
to the mystical powers of the birch tree under which the wizard
Merlin prophesied the Welsh victory over the Saxons.*

Fine-haired birch tree with white trunk—
You are bright—on the hillside,
God's hand planted where you are:
You're a cosy house for birds.
Like a nun under her veil,
You're bright beneath your red cowl.
Thick coils of silk from three branches
Are your green cap above the roads.

Merlin, the gifted poet—
You're very fair—sang to you:
Beneath your roof, pure fine dwelling,
He once sat composing verses,
And his distant sweet apple tree
Gave shelter to his little pig.

You got there—memorable battle—
Merlin's most learned knowledge.
Tell, birch below Pumlumon
Mountain, what rumors there are,
And how the world will turn out
In this time of provocation.

"Calamitious world of fierce pride,
Time of destruction for the strong;
And the world will lower its head,
And the offspring of Rowena's line,"
Merlin the magician said,
"The wheel will turn before this ebbs.
I know they will very soon—
Abhorent way—leave the faith.
They don't respect—they kill faith—
The kinship laws in marriage,
Nor relations nor lineage
Nor god-parenthood, worse still.
They praise not god without malice,
And leave not falsehood and harshness.
Pride is everywhere present,
And lies are commoner than truth.
There's more praise for sins after death
Than for getting to heaven.
Their poison has burgeoned
And their own deceit melts them.
The saints—well honored in their land—
And God close by are angry:
God's vengeance will be seen
On them, and famine indeed."

—WALES, C. 1395–1486

Loyalty

A strong sense of loyalty was an integral part of the Celtic character since the Iron Age. Their tribal society ensured that the Celts were devoted to the other people within their clans. Because each member of a clan was responsible for the others' actions, including their crimes, loyalty was crucial to individual esteem, societal order, and the quest for excellence in craftsmanship.

In literature, loyalty to family, friends, and lovers was one of the most crucial qualities one could possess. In the poems of *The Dean of Lismore*, a loyal warrior would follow a friend into battle without question and go to any lengths to save him from an enemy. In the Welsh epic, *The Mabinogion*, Teirnon's loyalty to Pwyll gains him great reward, but like all Celtic heroes, he considers his devotion to be its own reward.

From *The Mabinogion:*

Pwyll and Rhiannon ruled Dyved prosperously the first year and the second. The third year, however, the men of Dyved began to fret at seeing that this man whom they loved as their lord and foster-brother was still childless; consequently they summoned Pwyll to a meeting in Presseleu. "Lord, we realize you are not as old as some men in the land, but we fear your wife will never bear you a child. Take another woman so that you may have an heir. You will not last forever, and though you may wish matters to remain as they are, we will not permit it." "Well, even now we have not been together long, and much may yet happen," answered

Pwyll. "Give me another year; at the end of that time we will meet again and I will accept your advice." They set a date, and before the year was up Rhiannon bore Pwyll a son in Arberth. On the night of his birth women were brought in to look after mother and child, but these women and Rhiannon all fell asleep. Six women had been brought into the chamber, and they did watch for part of the night, but they were asleep before midnight and woke only at dawn; upon waking they searched round where they had left the boy, but there wasn't a trace of him. "Alas! The boy is lost!" said one woman. "Yes," said another, "and they would consider it getting off lightly if we were only burned or executed." "Is there any hope for us?" "There is—I have a good plan." "What is it?" they all asked. "There is a deerhound here with pups. We can kill some of the pups, smear Rhiannon's hands and face with the blood, throw the bones before her and insist that she destroyed her own child—it will be her word against that of us six." They settled on this plan.

Towards daybreak Rhiannon woke and asked, "Women, where is the child?" "Lady, do not ask us for the lad; we are nothing but blows and bruises from struggling with you, and we are certain that we have never seen such fight in any woman, so that all our struggling was in vain." "Poor souls," said Rhiannon, "by the Lord God who knows all things, do not accuse me falsely. God who knows all things knows your words are false. If you are afraid, by my confession to God, I will protect you." "God knows that we will not bring harm on ourselves for anyone's sake." "Poor souls, you will come to no harm for telling the truth." But whether her words were kind or pleading, Rhiannon got only the one answer from the women.

At this Pwyll Head of Annwvyn rose, with his company and his retinue, and the incident could not be kept from them. The story went round the land and all the nobles heard it, and they assembled and sent to Pwyll to ask him to separate from his wife because of the terrible outrage she had committed. Pwyll answered, "You have no reason to ask me to put away my wife, except for her being childless, and since I know that she has borne a child I will not part from her. If she has done wrong, let her be punished." Rhiannon summoned teachers and wise men, and as she preferred being punished to arguing with the women, she accepted her punishment. She had to remain for seven years at the court of Arberth, where she was to sit every day by the mounting-block near the gate and tell her story to anyone who might not already know it; she was also to offer to carry guests and strangers to the court on her back, though it was seldom that anyone let himself be so transported. Rhiannon spent part of a year thus.

At that time the lord of Gwent Ys Coed was Teirnon Twrvliant, la the best man in the world. Teirnon had a mare in his house, and there was not a handsomer horse in the realm. Every May Eve she foaled, but no one ever knew anything of the colt, so that Teirnon, in talking one night with his wife, said, "Wife, we are fools to lose the foal of our mare every year without getting even one of them." "What can you do about it?" "It is May Eve tonight," said he. "God's revenge on me if I do not find out what fate the foals have met with." So he had the mare brought inside, while he armed himself and began to watch. As night fell the mare foaled, a big colt without a flaw and standing already. Teirnon rose to remark the sturdiness of the colt, and as he did so he heard a great noise, whereupon a great daw came through the window and seized the colt by the mane. Teirnon drew his sword and hacked the arm off at the elbow, so that the colt and part of the arm were inside with him; hearing a loud crash and, simultaneously, a scream, he opened the door and rushed out after the noise, but the night was so dark he could see nothing. He was about to rush off and follow when he remembered that he had left the door open, and when he returned, he found by the door a small boy in swaddling clothes and wrapped in a silk mantle. Teirnon picked up the lad and observed that he was strong for his age; then he closed the door and made for his wife's chamber. "Lady, are you asleep?" "No, lord; I was, but I woke as you came in." "Here is a boy for you, if you want him, for that is the one thing you have never had." "Lord, what story is this?" she asked, so he told her what had happened. "See, lord, what kind of cloth is this the boy is wrapped in?" "A brocade mantle." "Then he is the son of noble folk. Lord, if you approve, this could be a joy and a comfort to me. I will take some women into my confidence, and we will let out that I have been pregnant." "I will gladly agree to that," said Teirnon. This was done. The boy was baptized in the manner usual for that time, and was given the name Gwri Golden Hair, because what hair was on his head was as yellow as gold. He was brought up at the court, and before he was a year old he could walk and was sturdier than a well-grown three-year-old. At the end of the second year he was as strong as a six-year-old, and by the time he was four he was bargaining with the stableboys to let him water the horses. "Lord," said Teirnon's wife, "where is the colt you rescued on the night you found the boy?" "I gave it into the care of the stableboys," answered Teirnon, "and ordered it to be looked after." "Would it not be a good idea to have it broken in and given to the boy? After all, you found the lad on the same night that the colt was born and rescued." "I will not argue against that—I will let you give it to him." "God reward you, lord, I will do that." So the horse was given to the lad, and Teirnon's wife went to the stableboys and grooms to command them to look after the colt and break it in for when the boy would go riding and there would be a story about him. Meanwhile they heard the news of Rhiannon and her punishment, and because of the find he had made, Teirnon listened to all the tales and made constant inquiries, so that he heard from those who came from Arberth numerous laments over Rhiannon's misfortune and disgrace. He thought over these accounts and looked closely at the boy, and it was clear to him that as regards appearance he had never seen father and son who resembled each other so much as did Pwyll Head of Annwvyn and this lad. Pwyll's appearance was well known to Teirnon, who had once been his man; thus as Teirnon looked now he was seized by anxiety, for he realized how wrong it was to keep a boy whom he knew to be another's son. As soon as he was alone with his wife, Teirnon told her it was not right for them to keep the lad and allow so noble a lady as Rhiannon to be punished when the boy was actually Pwyll's son. His wife agreed to send Gwri back to Pwyll, "for we will gain in three ways, lord: thanks and gratitude for releasing Rhiannon from her punishment, Pwyll's thanks for rearing the boy and returning him, and finally, if the boy grows into a good man, he will be our foster son and will always do the best he can for us." So they decided to give the boy back.

No later than the next day Teirnon and three companions equipped themselves and set out, with the boy as a fourth on the horse Teirnon had given him, and made for Arberth, and it wasn't long before they arrived. When they reached the court they saw Rhiannon sitting by the mounting-block, and as they drew near she said, "Chieftain, come no nearer. I will carry each one of you to the court, since that is my punishment for killing my son and destroying him with my own hands." "Lady," answered Teirnon, "I do not suppose any of us will allow you to carry him." "Let him be carried who will," said the boy, "but I will not." "God knows, friend, none of us will," said Teirnon. When they entered the court there was great rejoicing at their arrival. A feast was about to begin; Pwyll himself had just returned from a circuit of Dyved, so they all went in to wash, and Pwyll was glad to see Teirnon. They sat down thus: Teirnon between Pwyll and Rhiannon, and his two companions above Pwyll with the boy between them. After the first course everyone began to talk and carouse, and Teirnon told the tale of the mare and the boy, how the latter had been in the care of himself and his wife and how they had brought him up, and he said to Rhiannon, "Lady, look upon your son, for whoever lied about you did wrong. When I heard of your grief I was sorrowful and griefstricken myself. I do not suppose that anyone in this company will deny that the lad is Pwyll's son." "No, we have no doubt that he is," they all said. "Between me and God," said Rhiannon, "what a relief from my anxiety if all this is true." "Lady, you have named your son well," said the chieftain of Dyved, "for Pryderi son of Pwyll Head of Annwvyn is the name which suits him best." Rhiannon answered, "Ask if his own name does not suit him better." "What was his name?" asked the chieftain of Dyved. "We called him Gwri Golden Hair." "Then Pryderi should be his name," said the chieftain of Dyved, and Pwyll said, "It is right to name the boy after what his mother said when she received good news of him." So they named him Pryderi. Then Pwyll said, "Teirnon, God reward you for bringing up the boy all this time. If he grows into a good man he too ought to reward you." "Lord, my wife reared the boy, and no one in the world could grieve more over losing him than she does. He ought to remember, for my sake and hers, what we have done for him." "Between me and God," said Pwyll, "I will maintain both you and your land, so long as I am alive and able to maintain myself, and if he lives, it would be more fitting that he support you. If you and these nobles agree, since you have reared him until now, we will send him to be fostered by the chieftain of Dyved henceforth, and you shall all be companions and foster-fathers to him." Everyone agreed that this was a good idea, so the boy was given to the chieftain of Dyved and the nobles all allied themselves with him. Teirnon and his companions then set out for their own land and dominions, amid gladness and rejoicing; Teirnon did not leave without being offered the finest jewels and the best horses and dogs, but he would accept nothing.

—WALES, 14TH CENTURY

Here Caoilte Mac Ronan declares his loyalty to the hero Finn in
The Dean of Lismore:

I set me off to rescue Finn,
To Taura of the joyful streams;
With arms sure of victory,
To Cormac, son of Art Aonir.
I will not put forth my strength,
Though bloody and light of foot,
Until that with Feinn of Fail,
We have reached the shore of Loch Foyle.
Then we did slay the mighty hero,
Then we had slain Cuireach.
We killed a mighty warrior
When we had killed their leader.
We bore his head up to the hill,
Which lies above Buadhamair.
Then indeed I had my triumph,
For I made a total havoc.
For the hero's sake I slew
A man in every town in Erin.
Then indeed I had my triumph,
For I made a total havoc
The calves I slew with the cows,
Whom I found in all fair Erin.
Then indeed I had my triumph,
For I made a total havoc.
The doors on which the red wind blew,
I threw them each one widely open.
Then indeed I had my triumph,
For I made a total havoc.
The fields all ripe throughout the land,
I set them then a blazing brightly.

Then indeed I had my triumph,
For I made a total havoc.
In my day there won't be seen
Either miln or kiln in Erin.

—SCOTLAND 16TH CENTURY

From *The Dean Of Lismore:*

*Here, a warrior declares his love for the hero Finn Mac Cumhail,
and swears that he would follow him anywhere:*

SWEET is a man's voice in the land of gold,
Sweet the sounds the birds produce,
Sweet is the murmur of the crane,
Sweet sound the waves at Bun Datreor,
Sweet the soft murmuring of the wind,
Sweet sounds the cuckoo at Cas a choin.
How soft and pleasing shines the sun,
Sweet the blackbird sings his song;
Sweet the eagle's voice of Easaroy,
Above the sea of great MacMorn;
Sweet the cuckoo 'mongst the branches,
Sweet the silence of the crane.
Finn Mac Cumhail is my father,
Who nobly leads the Feinn's seven bands;
When he his hounds lets loose to hunt,
To follow him is truly sweet.
Sweet.

—ANONYMOUS, SCOTLAND, 16TH CENTURY

The Otherworld

"The belief of Pythagoras is strong in them, that souls of men are immortal, and that after a definite number of years they live a second life when the soul passes to another body. This is the reason given why some people at the burial of the dead cast upon the pyre letters written to their dead relatives, thinking that the dead will be able to read them."

—Diodorus Siculus, on the Celtic belief in life after death

In the Celtic world, the living and the dead—supernatural beings from the Otherworld—often lived side by side. Visitors from the Otherworld (or the "afterlife") often entered the real world in the form of an animal, while humans were able to enter the supernatural realm easily—although not without adverse consequences. The journey of a mortal into the Otherworld could prove to be dangerous, particularly in the Arthurian legends, in which Arthur's quest for a magical cauldron costs the lives of his men.

In Irish myth, the Otherworld is portrayed as a land of milk and honey, where beautiful music, mead, and women reign supreme. *The Voyage of Bran* chronicles the journey of Bran son of Febral to the Otherworld, and is one of the most vivid accounts of the Celtic concept of the afterlife. In the story, when the hero grabs the apple branch—a symbol of the entrance to the spiritual world— he embarks on a quest for the Land of Women, a realm where hospitality knows no bounds and endless pleasures await.

In the myth *St. Patrick's Purgatory,* the journey to the Otherworld becomes a path to holiness. According to legend, St. Patrick entered the world of the dead at Lough Derg, County Donegal. The legend was related by the twelfth century monk Henry of Saltey, who heard the story from Owen, a knight who made a pilgrimage to Purgatory. It is believed that the story of St. Patrick's journey to the Otherworld would go on to influence Dante's *Inferno*. According to Renan, "The Purgatory of St. Patrick became the framework of another series of tales embodying the Celtic ideas concerning the other life and its different states. . . . In the fact of the unknown that lies beyond the tomb, they dream of that great journey which the pen of Dante has celebrated." And Frederick Vinton confirms in his *Biblia Sacra:* "In some of these forms these legends must have fallen under the eyes of Dante."

> From *The Voyage Of Bran:*
>
> *One of the most celebrated Otherworld tales in Celtic literature,* The Voyage of Bran *embodies the Celtic belief that the afterlife was a glorious place, filled with sensual pleasures. In tales of the Otherworld journey, the hero is given an apple branch, which permits his entry into a world beyond time and space. In this selection, we discover how Bran first enters the Otherworld, where renewal can begin.*

'TWAS fifty quatrains the woman from unknown lands sang on the floor of the house to Bran son of Febral, when the royal house was full of kings, who knew not whence the woman had come, since the ramparts where closed.

This is the beginning of the story. One day, in the neighborhood of his stronghold, Bran went about alone, when he heard music behind him. As often as he looked back, 'twas still behind him the music was. At last he fell asleep at the music, such was its sweetness. When he awoke from his sleep, he saw close behind a branch of silver with white blossoms, nor was it easy to distinguish its bloom from that branch. Then Bran took the branch in his hand to his royal house. When the hosts were in the royal house, they saw a woman in strange raiment on the floor of the house. 'Twas then she sang the fifty quatrains to Bran, while the host heard her, and all beheld the woman.

And she said:

A branch of the apple-tree from Emain
I bring, like those one knows;
Twigs of white silver are on it,
Crystal brows with blossoms,

There is a distant isle,
Around which sea-horses glisten;
A fair course against the white-swelling surge—
Four feet uphold it.

A delight of the eyes, a glorious range,
Is the plain on which the hosts hold games:
Coracle contends against chariot
In southern Mag Findargat.

Feet of white bronze under it
Glittering through beautiful ages.
Lovely land thoughout the world's age,
On which many blossoms drop.

An ancient tree there is with blossoms,
On which birds call to the Hours.
'Tis in harmony it is their wont
To call together every Hour.

Splendours of every color glisten
Throughout the gentle-voiced plains.
Joy is known, ranked around music,
In southern Mag Argatnel.

Unknown is wailing or treachery
In the familiar cultivated land,
There is nothing rough or harsh,
But sweet music striking on the ear.

Without grief, without sorrow, without death,
Without any sickness, without debility,
That is the sign of Emain—
Uncommon is an equal marvel.

A beauty of a wondrous land,
Whose aspects are lovely,
Whose view is a fair country,
Incomparable is its haze.

Then if Aircthech is seen,
On which dragonstones and crystals drop
The sea washes the wave against the land,
Hair of crystal drops from its mane.

Wealth, treasures of every hue,
Are in Ciuin, a beauty of freshness,
Listening to sweet music,
Drinking the best of wine.

Golden chariots in Mag Rein,
Rising with the tide to the sun,

Chariots of silver in Mag Mon,
And of bronze without blemish.

Yellow golden steeds are on the sward there,
Other steeds with crimson hue,
Others with wool upon their backs
Of the hue of heaven all-blue.

At sunrise there will come across the clear sea,
A fair man illumining level lands;
He rides upon the fair sea-washed plain,
He stirs the ocean till it is blood.

A host will come across the clear sea,
To the land they show their rowing;
Then they row to the conspicuous stone,
From which arise a hundred strains.

It sings a strain unto the host
Through long ages, it is not sad,
Its music swells with choruses of hundreds—
They look for neither decay nor death.

Many-shaped Emne by the sea,
Whether it be near, whether it be far,
In which are many thousands of motley women
Which the clear sea encircles.

If he has heard the voice of the music,
The chorus the little birds from Imchiuin,
A small band of women will come from a height
To the plain of sport in which he is.

There will come happiness with health,
To the land against which laughter peals,
Into Imchiuin at every season
Will come everlasting joy.

—IRELAND, 8TH CENTURY

The Founding of the Purgatory:

This fifteenth century English poem recounts Knight Owen's journey into St. Patrick's Purgatory. In this selection, we discover how Patrick came to enter the Otherworld.

Christ spake to St. Patrick then
By name he bade with him go,
He led him into a wilderness.
There neither man nor beast was
And showed him that well he might see
Into the earth a privy entry.
It was in a deep dark's end;
That man, said he, that would have here inwend
And dwell herein a day and a night
And how he is behaved alright,
And come again, note he will
Marvelous tales may he tell.
What man goeth this pilgrimage,
I shall him grant for his wage
Be it man woman or knave
Other Purgatory shall he never have.
As soon as he went to him and said so
Jesu went that Bishop from.
Saint Patrick went anon right
He stood not day nor night,
But get him help from day to day,
And did make theirs a rich abbey

Regles that hath the same day.
Saint Patrick did make full well
A door bounden with iron and steel;
Lock and key he made there too;
That no man should that door undo;
The key he took to the Prior
And bade him lock as his treasure.
There he locked the entry too
That no man might therein go,
But if he were at the assent
Of the prior and his convent,
Yet from the Bishop he must have a letter
Or else he were never the better.
Yet is this stead in rememory
Cleped Saint Patrick's Purgatory.
In his time some were therein
To get forgiveness of their sin
And come again all on the morrow,
God with them, told of mickle sorrow,
Of pains that they seen there
And of mickle joy also.
What they seen well they wete
For they have in books writ.
Some went in bolder were
And come again never more.
In Steve's time I understand
That there was a knight in England
A knight there was men cleped Sir Owen,
He was therein and come again;
What he saw there I will you tell
Both of Heaven and of Hell.

—ENGLAND, C. A.D. 1400

From *Oisin in Tír na nÓg:*

According to legend, Oisin, son of Finn Mac Cumhail and one of the great poets and heroes of ancient Ireland, lived to the time of St. Patrick, two hundred years past his fellow warriors in the Fena. In the following story, we discover how Oisin lived to such a ripe old age. Here he explains to St. Patrick that after fighting in the great Battle of Gabhra, in which his fellow warriors were destroyed, he was saved by a fairy, Niamh of the Golden Hair. She takes him to Tír na nÓg, "the Land of Youth" or the Fairy Otherworld, where he is healed and celebrated as a great warrior.

A short time after the final Battle of Gabhra where so many of our heroes fell, we were hunting on a dewy morning near the brink of Loch Lein, where the trees and hedges around us were all fragrant with blossoms, and the little birds sang melodious music on the branches. We soon roused the deer from the thickets, and as they bounded over the plain, our hounds followed after them in full cry.

We were not so long engaged, when we saw a rider coming swiftly towards us from the west; and we soon perceived that it was a maiden on a white steed. We all ceased from the chase on seeing a lady, who reined in as she approached. And Finn and the Fena were greatly surprised, for they had never before seen so lovely a maiden. A slender golden diadem encircled her head; and she wore a brown robe of silk, spangled with stars of red gold, which was fastened in front by a golden brooch, and fell from her shoulders till it swept the ground. Her yellow hair flowed far down over her robe in bright, golden ringlets. Her blue eyes were as clear as the drops of dew on the grass; and while her small white hand held the bridle and curbed her steed with a golden bit, she sat more gracefully than the swan on Loch Lein. The white steed was covered with a smooth, flowing mantle. He was shod with four shoes of pure yellow gold, and in all Erin a better or more beautiful steed could not be found.

As she came to the presence of Finn, he addressed her courteously: "Who art thou, O lovely youthful princess? Tell us thy name and the name of thy country, and relate to us the cause of thy coming."

She answered in a sweet and gentle voice: "Noble king of the Fena, I have had a long journey this day, for my country lies far off in the Western Sea. I am the daughter of the king of Tír na nÓg, and my name is Niamh of the Golden Hair."

"And what is it that has caused thee to come so far across the sea? Has thy husband forsaken thee; or what other evil has befallen thee?"

"My husband has not forsaken me, for I have never been married or betrothed to any man. But I love thy noble son, Oisin: and this is what has brought me to Erin. It is not without reason that I have given him my love, and that I have undertaken this long journey: for I have often heard of his bravery, his gentleness, and the nobleness of his person. Many princes and high chiefs have sought me in marriage; but I was quite indifferent to all men, and never consented to wed, till my heart was moved with love for thy gentle son, Oisin."

When I heard these words, and when I looked on the lovely maiden with her glossy, golden hair, I was all over in love with her. I came near, and, taking her small hand in mine, I told her she was a mild star of brightness and beauty, and that I preferred her to all the princesses in the world for my wife.

"Then," said she, "I place you under geasa, which true heroes never break through, to come with me on my white steed to Tír na nÓg, the land of never-ending youth. It is the most delightful land and the most renowned country under the sun. There is an abundance of gold and silver and jewels, of honey and wine; and the trees bear fruit and blossoms and green leaves together all the year round. You will get a hundred swords and a hundred robes of silk and satin, a hundred swift steeds, and a hundred slender, keen-scenting hounds. You will get herds of cows without number and flocks of sheep with fleeces of gold; a coat of mail that cannot be pierced, and a sword than never missed a stroke and from which no one ever escaped alive. There are feasting and harmless pastimes each day. A hundred warriors fully armed shall always await you at call, and harpers shall delight you with their sweet music. You will wear the diadem of the king of Tír na nÓg, which he never gave to any one under the sun, and which will guard you day and night, in tumult and battle and danger of every kind. Lapse of time shall bring neither decay nor death, and you shall be forever young, and gifted with unfading beauty and strength. All these delights you shall enjoy, and many others that I do not mention; and I myself will be your wife if you come with me to Tír na nÓg."

—IRELAND, FIRST WRITTEN DOWN C. 8TH CENTURY

Souls from the Otherworld often entered the real world to warn the living of impending danger. In The Death of Arthur *by Chrétien de Troyes, Sir Gawain comes to King Arthur from the Otherworld and warns him that he must call off the battle with Mordred, or he will face certain death.*

On the eve of the battle, King Arthur had a dream. He thought he sat crowned in his royal robes; his throne was a mighty wheel. He looked down, and below him saw a black water, wherein dragons swam. The king shuddered, lest he should fall among those fiends, who fought with one another; on a sudden, the wheel went round and every dragon seized him by a limb. Arthur shrieked, as if he would go mad; his chamberlains ran and roused him. All night he waked, with sad heart, in his tent lit with many tapers; toward morn, he fell asleep. By a broad and deep river he saw Sir Gawain, with an unnumbered host, shining like angels from heaven. Never was the king so blithe as when his nephew he saw. "Welcome, Sir Gawain! If thou livest, well for me! Tell me, dear friend, hide it not, who are the folk that follow thee?" "Sir, these are they who bide in bliss where I dwell. Lords and ladies were they, who have lost the life of this world; when I was a man, I fought for their sakes; now I find them my dearest friends; they bless the day that I was born, and leave they have asked with me to wend, that they might meet you here. A month's truce must you take, ere you array yourself for battle; Lancelot of the Lake cometh to your aid, with many a man of worth; today you must not fight, or else shall you be slain."

The king woke and wept: "Alas, the sad sound!" In haste he dight on his robes, and to his lords he cried: "Alas, I have been in deep dreams, so that naught can give me joy; we must send to Sir Mordred, and choose another time, or else be undone; this I learned, as in bed I lay. Go, Sir Lucan, thou who hast wise words at command, and take with thee bishops and bold barons."

—FRANCE, C.A.D. 1140

Prophecy

An accurate prophecy in the Celtic world had the capability to warn when impending enemies were near or if one's own death was imminent. The ancient Druids went to great lengths to attain this ability, and believed that by drinking the blood of a bull, they would fall into a deep sleep in which visions of the future would be revealed. It was also common for supernatural beings from the Otherworld to appear in a prophetic dream with a warning. In the Arthurian legends, King Arthur is warned of his own death when he is visited by his friend Gawain from the Otherworld.

From *The Yellow Book Of Lecan:*

In literature, an accurate prophecy had the power to save an entire country, as in The Yellow Book of Lecan. *Sualtaim's warning to Conchobar and the other men of Ulster rescues Ireland from a certain catastrophe.*

The Long Warning Of Sualtaim

While the things that we have related were done, Suallaith heard from Rath Sualtaim in Mag Murthemne the vexing of his son Cuchulainn against twelve sons of Gaile Dana and his sister's son. It is then that Sualtaim said:

"Is it heaven that bursts, or the sea over its boundaries, or earth that is destroyed, or the shout of my son against odds?"

Then he comes to his son. Cuchulainn was displeased that he should come to him. "Though he were slain, I should not have

169

strength to avenge him. Go to the Ulstermen," says Cuchulainn, "and let them give battle to the warriors at once; if they do not give it, they will not be avenged for ever."

When his father saw him, there was not in his chariot as much as the point of a rush would cover that was not pierced. His left hand which the shield protected, twenty wounds were in it.

Sualtaim came over to Emain and shouted to the Ulstermen: "Men are being slain, women carried off, cows driven away!"

His first shout was from the side of the court; his second from the side of the fortress; the third shout was on the mound of the hostages in Emain. No one answered; it was the practice of the Ulstermen that none of them should speak except to Conchobar; and Conchobar did not speak before the three Druids.

"Who takes them, who steals them, who carries them off?" said the Druid.

"Ailill Mac Mata carries them off and steals them and takes them, through the guidance of Fergus Mac Roich," said Sualtaim. "Your people have been enslaved as far as Dun Sobairce; their cows and their women and their cattle have been taken. Cuchulainn did not let them into Mag Murthemne and into Crich Rois; three months of winter then, bent branches of hazel held together his dress upon him. Dry wisps are on his wounds. He has been wounded so that he has been parted joint from joint."

"Fitting," said the Druid, "were the death of the man who has spurred on the king."

"It is fitting for him," said Conchobar.

"It is fitting for him," said the Ulstermen.

"True is what Sualtaim says," said Conchobar; "from the Monday night of Samhain to the Monday night of Candlemas he has been in this foray."

Sualtaim gave a leap out thereupon. He did not think sufficient the answer that he had. He falls on his shield, so that the engraved edge of the shield cut his head off. His head is brought back into Emain into the house on the shield, and the head says the same word (though some say that he was asleep on the stone, and that he fell thence on to his shield in awaking).

"Too great was this shout," said Conchobar. "The sea before them, the heaven over their tops, the earth under their feet. I will bring every cow into its milking-yard, and every woman and every boy from their house, after the victory in battle."

Then Conchobar struck his hand on his son, Findchad Fer m-Bend. Hence he is so called because there were horns of silver on him.

"Arise, O Findchad, I will send thee to Deda,"

It was not difficult for Findchad to take his message, for they were, the whole province of Conchobar, every chief of them, awaiting Conchobar; every one was then east and north and west of Emain. When they were there, they all came till they were at Emain Macha. When they were there, they heard the uprising of Conchobar in Emain. They went past Emain southwards after the host. Their first march then was from Emain to Irard Cuillend.

"What are you waiting for here?" said Conchobar.

"Waiting for your sons," said the host. "They have gone with thirty with them to Temair to seek Eirc, son of Coirpre Niafer and Fedelm Noicride. Till their two cantreds should come to us, we will not go from this place."

"I will not remain indeed," said Conchobar, "till the men of Ireland know that I have awaked from the sickness in which I was."

Conchobar and Celtchar went with three fifties of chariots, and they brought eight twenties of heads from Ath Airthir Midi; hence is Ath Fene. They were there watching the host. And eight twenties of women, that was their share of the spoil. Their heads were brought there, and Conchobar and Celtchar sent them to the camp. It is there that Celtchar said to Conchobar: (Or it was Cuscraid, the Stammerer of Macha, son of Conchobar, sang this song the night before the battle, after the song which Loegaire Buadach had sung, to wit, "Arise, kings of Macha," etc., and it would be in the camp it was sung.)

It was in this night that the vision happened to Dubthach Doeltenga of Ulster, when the hosts were on Garach and Irgarach. It is there that he said in his sleep: "A wonder of a morning, a wonder of a time, when hosts will be confused, kings will be turned, necks will break, the sun will grow red, three hosts will be routed by the track of a host about Conchobar. They will strive for their women, they will chase their flocks in fight on the morning, heroes will be smitten . . ."

—IRELAND, 8TH CENTURY

The Role of Women

"In fact, a whole band of foreigners will be unable to cope with them in a fight, if he calls in his wife, stronger than he by far and with flashing eyes; least of all when she swells her neck and flashes her teeth, and poising her huge white arms, begins to rain blows mingled with kicks, like shots, discharged by the twisted cords of a catapult."

—Ammanius Marcellinus (c. 330–391), on the ferocity and skill of ancient Celtic women warriors on the battlefield

In their social history, literature, and law, the ancient Celts displayed a remarkably progressive and democratic attitude toward women, even by modern standards. The historian Diodorus Siculus was particularly struck by the ability of Celtic women on the battlefield, remarking: "Gaulish women are not only equal to men in size, but they are a match for them in strength as well." In *The Táin*, women are the fiercest warriors and the most defiant leaders. Scathach, the female Amazonian warrior, is responsible for Cuchulainn's training in battle. It is she who teaches him martial arts as well as his trademark leap, the thunderfeat. Similarly, Queen Medb, the warrior queen of Connacht and the leading figure in *The Ulster Cycle*, holds unwavering power over men both with her courage and with her potent sexual allure. The very sight of her is said to deprive men of their strength, and in *The Táin* she demonstrates defiance towards her husband, Ailill, when she tells him that it is *her* accomplishments and reputation that have brought fortune and glory to their marriage, not his. It is also Medb who leads the Connacht forces into battle, and although she is not always proven to act prudently while in battle, she does prove a worthy adversary to Cuchulainn. In *The Mabinogion*, women are responsible for ruling along with their husbands, as well as aiding them against their enemies. In Irish history, the very personification of Ireland is Grainuaile, based on Grainne Ni Mhaille (c. 1530–1603), the fierce, seafaring heroine of the sixteenth century who defied Queen Elizabeth I and was unbeatable in battle.

This egalitarian view of women is particularly apparent in the Brehon Laws (the ancient laws of Ireland), especially in the household. The rights of a woman were dependent upon the income that she brought to the house, and she proved to be an equal partner in raising children and deciding the budget. The Brehon Laws also introduced the idea of equal pay for equal work, a concept that modern societies are still struggling to realize. It is apparent that the comparatively equal position that women held in Celtic societies empowered them to become strong leaders and warriors. While no society is utopian, it is remarkable that the position of women upheld in ancient Celtic practice seems visionary even today.

In this selection from The Táin, Cuchulainn's Courtship of Emer, *the hero Cuchulainn receives his training in arms from the master, the Amazon warrior Scathach.*

Then Uathach came and conversed with Cuchulain. On the third day she advised him, if it were to achieve valor that he had come, that he should go through the hero's salmon leap to reach Scathach, in the place where she was teaching her two sons, Cuar and Cett, in the great yew-tree; that he should set his sword between her breasts until she yielded him his three wishes; namely to teach him without neglect; that without payment of wedding gifts he might wed Uathach; and that she should fortell his future, for she was a prophetess.

Cuchulain then went to the place where Scathach was. He placed his two feet on the edges of the basket of the feats, and bared his sword, and put its point to her heart, saying, "Death hangs over thee!" "Name thy three demands!" said she; "thy three demands, as thou canst utter them in one breath."

"They must be fulfilled," said Cuchulain. And he pledged her. Uathach then was given to Cuchulain, and Scathach taught him skill of arms.

—IRELAND, 8TH CENTURY

In one of the most famous and engaging passages from The Táin, *entitled* Pillow Talk, *Medb (meaning "the intoxicating one" in Irish, as indeed she proves herself to be), rides roughshod over her beleaguered husband, Ailill, and asserts her superior position in their marriage.*

Once of a time that Ailill and Medb had spread their royal bed in Cruachan fort in Connacht, such was the pillow-talk that fell before them:

Quoth Ailill "True is the saying lady," Ailill said, "She is a well-off woman that is a rich man's wife."

"Aye, that she is," answered the wife. "But wherefore opin'st so?"

"For this," Ailill said, "that thou art this day better off than the day that I first took thee."

"As well-ff was I before I ever saw thee," Medb said.

"It was a wealth forsooth, we never knew nor heard of," Ailill said, "but a woman's wealth was all thou hadst, and foes from lands next thine were used to carry off the spoil and booty that they took from thee."

"Not so was I," Medb said, "the High King odf Erin himself was my sire—Eochaid Fedlech the enduringt, the son of Finn, the son of Findoman, the son of Finden, the son of Findguin, the son of Rogan Ruad, the son of Rigen, the son of Blathacht, the son of Beothacht, the son of Enna Agnech, the son of Oengus Turbech. Of daughters, he had six: Derbriu, Ethne, Ele, Clothru, Muguin, and myself Medb, myself, that was the noblest and seemliest of them. "Twas I the goodliest of them in bounty and gift giving in riches and in treasures. Twas I had fifteen hundred royal mercenaries of the sons of aliens, all exiles' sons, and as many more of the sons of freeman of the land. And there were ten men with every one of these hirelings and nine men with every hireling, and eight men with every hireling, and seven men with every hireling, and six men with every hireling, and five men with every hireling, and four men with every hireling, and two men with every hireling, and one hireling with every hireling."

"Hence hath my father bestowed on me one of the five provinces of Erin, even the province of Cruachan, wherefore 'Medb of Cruachan' am I called. Men came from Finn, son of Ross Ruad, the king of Leinster to woo me, and I refused him. And they came from Conchobar, king of Ulster, son of Fachtna, and they come from Eochaid Bec, and I refused him in like wise. And they came from Eocho Bec and I went not; for 'tis I exacted for a singular bride, such as no woman before me had ever required of a man of the men of Erin, namely, a husband without avarice, without jealousy, without fear."

"For should he be mean, the man with whom I should live, we were ill-matched together, inasmuch as I am great in largesse and gift-giving, and it would be a disgrace for my husband if I should be better at spending than he, and for it to be said that I was superior in wealth and treasures to him while no disgrace would it be were one as great as the other. Were my husband a coward 'twere as unfit for us to be matched, for I by myself and alone break battles and combats, and 'twould be a reproach for my husband should his wife be more full of life than himself, and no

reproach our being qually bold. Should he be jealous, the husband
with whom I should live, that would not suit me, for there never
was a time that I have not had my paramour."

—IRELAND, 8TH CENTURY

In this selection from The Battle of the Bulls, *Medb shows the
courage of a man on the battlefield, and yet we are still reminded
that she is undeniably female. We are also reminded that not all
men saw women warriors as equals, when Fergus insults Medb,
discounting her as "a misguiding woman."*

Medb had set up a shelter of shields to guard the rear of the
men in Ireland. She had sent off the Brown Bull of Cuailnge to
Cruachan by a roundabout road, with fifty of his heifers and eight
messengers so that, whoever escaped, the Brown Bull of Cuailnge
would be got safely away, as she had sworn.

Then Medb got her gush of blood.

"Fergus," she said, "take over the shelter of shields at the rear
of the men in Ireland until I relieve myself."

"By God," Fergus said, "you have picked a bad time for this."

"I can't help it," Medb said, "I'll die if I can't do it."

So Fergus took over the shelter of shields at the rear of the
men in Ireland and Medb relieved herself. She dug three great
channels, each big enough to take a household. The place is called
Fual Medba, Medb's Foul Place, ever since. Cuchulainn found her
like this, but he held his hand. He wouldn't strike her from behind.

"Spare me," Medb said.

"If I killed you dead," Cuchulainn said, "it would only be
right."

But he spared her, not being a killer of women. He watched
them all the way westward until they passed Ath Luain, and there
he stopped. He struck three blows of his sword at the stone hills

nearby. The Bald-Topped Hills is their name now, at Ath Luain, in answer to the three Bald-topped Hills in Meath.

The battle was over.

Medb said to Fergus: "We have a shame and a shambles here today, Fergus."

"We followed the rump of a misguiding woman," Fergus said, "It is the usual thing for a herd led by a mare to be strayed and destroyed."

—IRELAND, 8TH CENTURY

In these selections from the Brehon Laws, which may be the first to emphasize "equal pay for equal work," we see just how much power women had in ancient Irish society.

If a woman has the full work of a woman, whether it [the work] be productive or non-productive, she shall obtain [the value of] the full work of the man.

—IRELAND, C. A.D. 438

From *The Senchus Mor,* Law Of Social Connections:

In the connection of equal property, if with equal land and cattle and household stuff, and if their marriage be equally free and lawful, the wife in this case is called the wife of equal rank. The contract made by either party is not, in that case, a lawful contract without the consent of the other, except in case of contracts tending equally to the welfare of both; such as the alliance of co-tillage with a lawful tribe when they [the couple] have not the means themselves of doing the work of ploughing, the taking of land, the collecting of food, etc.

—IRELAND, C. A.D. 438

From *The Senchus Mor,* Law Of Social Connections:

If she be a woman of first lawful marriage, of equal property, and of equal family, she can disturb all the man's contracts, if they be ill advised, for legality cannot attach to fraud which is opposed: her sons may dissolve them.

—IRELAND, C. A.D. 438

From *The Senchus Mor,* Law Of Social Connections:

The sons and, if there are no sons, the daughters of their mother, claim a right to enter upon and take possession of the lands in respect to which legal contracts for full consideration and dealing with coibne land had been made for with their mother; for the geilfine chief, who must for this purpose be one of the geil-fine division, confirms [has confirmed] the contract.

—IRELAND, C. A.D. 438

In this passage from The Mabinogion, The Dream of Maxen, *we see the concept of courtly love and chivalry towards women introduced, when Maxen proves he will go to any length to please the woman he loves. In this selection, the emphasis moves from the woman as warrior to the woman as object of romance and affection.*

Maxen entered the fortress, and inside the hall he saw Kynon son of Eudav and Avaon son of Eudav playing gwyddbwyll, and Eudav son of Caradawg sitting in the ivory chair carving gwyddb-wyll pieces, and the girl from his dream sitting in the red gold chair.

"Hail to the Empress of Rome," he said, and he embraced her, and that night he slept with her. The next morning she asked for her gift, as he had found her a virgin, and he told her to name her own gift. She asked for the island of Britain for her father, from the English Channel to the Irish Sea, and the three offshore islands for the empress of Rome, and three strongholds to be made for her in the island of Britain, in the places she chose. She asked that the chief fortress be built in Arvon, and soil from

Rome was brought so that it would be healthier for the emperor to sit and sleep and move about. The other fortresses were none other than Caer Llion and Caer Vyrddin. One day Maxen went to hunt at Caer Vyrddin; he went to the top of Y Vrenni Vawr and pitched his tent there, and the tent ground has been known as Cadeir Vaxen ever since. Caer Vyrddin, on the other hand, was so called because it was built by a multitude of men. Afterwards, Elen thought to have highways built from one fortress to another across the island; these were built, and are now called the highways of Elen of the Hosts, because of her British origin—that is, because the men of the island would not have assembled for anyone but her.

—WALES, 14TH CENTURY

In this selection from Owein, or The Countess of the Fountain, *it is a woman who saves Owein's life, and is therefore rewarded with his love and friendship.*

Owein saw through the join of the gate a road, and a row of houses on each side of the road, and a girl with curly yellow hair and a gold headband, dressed in yellow brocade and wearing buskins of mottled cordovan. This girl approached the gate and asked for it to be opened. "God knows, lady," said Owein, "the gate will not be opened from out here, any more than you can rescue me from in there." "God knows, it is a shame that you cannot be rescued," answered the girl. "It would be right for a woman to help you, for God knows, I have never seen a better man for a woman than you. If you had a woman-friend she would be the best of woman-friends, and if you had a lover she would be the best of lovers; therefore I will do what I can to help you. Take this ring and put it on your finger, and keep the stone in your hand and close your fist over it, for as long as you conceal it, it will conceal you. Those in the castle will come to put you to death because of the man you killed, but when they do not see you they will be annoyed. I will wait for you by the mounting-block, and though I will not see you, you will see me; put your hand on my shoulder to tell me you have come, and then follow me." She left Owein, and he did what she had told him. Men came from the court to put him to death, but they saw only half a horse, and that annoyed them; meanwhile Owein slipped away and found the girl and put his hand on her shoulder, and she led him to the door of a large handsome upper chamber. She opened the door and they entered, and then she closed it behind them, and as Owein looked round he saw not a single nail uncoloured with a precious colour, and not a single plank without a different gold image. The girl kindled a fire with charcoal, then took a silver bowl with water in it and a towel of fine white linen on her shoulder and gave the water to Owein to wash. After that she set before him a gilded silver table with a cloth of yellow linen and brought him dinner; Owein was certain he had never seen any food which was not there in large quantity, and moreover the service was better than anywhere else. He had never seen so many excellent gifts of food and drink, nor was he served from cups other than of silver and gold. Owein ate and drank until evening, when he heard a crying out in the fortress, and he asked the girl, "What outcry is this?" "They are anointing the nobleman who owns this fortress," she answered. Then he went to sleep, and the bed she made up for him of scarlet and fur and brocade and fine linens was worthy of Arthur himself. Towards midnight they heard a frightful crying, and Owein asked, "What crying is this now?" "The nobleman who owns this fortress has just died." A short while after dawn they heard another cry and immeasurably loud shouting, and Owein asked, "What is the meaning of this shouting?" "They are taking the body of the nobleman who owns this fortress to church." Then Owein rose and dressed himself, and when he opened the chamber window and looked out at the fortress he saw neither end nor limit to the crowds which were filling the streets, and they were all armed; many women, both mounted and on foot, were there, and all the clergymen of the fortress were chanting, and he felt the air reverberate with the shouting and trumpeting and clergymen chanting. In the midst of this host was a bier covered with a cloth of white linen, round which many wax candles burned, while in the procession there was no man of lesser rank than baron. Owein was certain he had never seen a handsomer looking host in such brocade and silk and linen. There followed a woman whose yellow hair flowed over her shoulders and whose head was covered with many bloody wounds; she wore a torn outfit of yellow brocade and buskins of mottled cordovan, and it was a wonder that her fingertips did not break the way she wrung her hands together. Owein was certain that had she been herself he would never have seen such a beautiful woman. She cried more loudly than any man or horn of the host, and as he looked upon her he was kindled with a love that filled every part of him.

—WALES, 14TH CENTURY

From *The Dindshenchas:*

In this poem from The Dindshenchas, *the collection of ancient Irish legends recounting how famous heroes and places were named, we discover how Rath Esa ("Rath" meaning fort in Irish, and thought to refer to fairy dwellings) earned its name. In this selection, women warriors fight alongside the men to rescue Esa, the daughter of Étain.*

Here settled as we believe,
After an eager coming to the gaol,
The daughter of Eochu Airem
And of Étain the noble.

Esa was the name of the maid,
From her is Rath Esa called:

A hundred of every [sort of] beast without abatement
Were brought by her who was best in havior.

Midir kept the fair woman
With wine and mead to drink;
Nine years did the maiden spend
At Bri Leith, spot of the waves.

In spite of Eochu Airem
Midir bore off Étain over the wine
From Fremand, though it was a bright country;
So she left Banba the mournful.

Said Codal of the withered foot:
"You need not search for her;
[Look] in Bri Leith in the very first place;
'Tis thither she has gone a-wooing."

By the side of Eochu Airem
Came the hosts of noble Erin
From Fremand, though it was a bright country,
To sack bright Bri Leth.

Nine years were they about this sacking;
Its speed was not very great.
Midir kept repulsing them
[And] kept destroying their works.

After the sack of the fairy fort
There came fifty hardy men,
(Transshaped was this tribe)
To talk with the slaughtering kings.

Then were brought on a Wednesday
('Twas a famous tale I heard)
To Eochu in the form of Étain,
Three score of women, a victorious force.

—IRELAND, C. A.D. 1150

Sexuality

"The result of ignoring women in law codes is that wealth will be overly desired in such a state, especially if women run things behind the scenes as in most military societies. An exception to this would be those nations which openly approve of sexual relations between men, such as the Celts and certain others."

—Aristotle, on the openness of sexuality between Celtic warriors

One of the most remarkable characteristics of pre-Christian Celtic societies was the absolute sexual freedom afforded both men and women. According to the classical writers, there was also a lack of inhibition regarding same-sex relationships, as Diodorus Siculus observed: "The women of the Gauls are very beautiful, but nevertheless, the men strongly prefer to have sex with other males." We see this disregard for sexual taboos contantly in Celtic literature, where there is a complete absence of inhibition about the number of sexual partners and the amount of activity. Even mothers often encourage their daughters to sleep with men if they are attracted to them. In *The Táin,* Scathach gives her blessing to her daughter Uathach without reservation when she sees a man she wants to seduce. In the early Irish myths, men have no compunction about sleeping with another man's wife.

The sexual permissiveness that pervades Celtic literature would seem to have a direct correlation to the great freedom granted to women in Celtic societies. Because women had equal rights in the home and on the battlefield, they gained an equal place in the bedroom. The female warriors like Queen Medb used both their force and their sexuality to conquer their male enemies, and displayed a libido that rivaled their male counterparts.

From *Cuchulainn's Courtship of Emer and His Training in Arms:*

Ancient Irish mothers, unlike the ones of today, wisely encouraged their daughters to take men to bed. In this selection from The Táin, we see the perfect example of Celtic motherly advice, when Scathach advises her daughter to pursue her lust for a young man.

She [Scathach] sent her daughter Uathach out to meet the young man and see who he might be. Uathach saw him and fell silent, his sweet shape woke such desire in her. She gazed her fill at him and them went back to her mother. She told her mother about the man she had seen and praised him.

"I can see he pleases you." Her mother said.

"Yes indeed," the girl said.

"Take him to bed tonight," she said, "and sleep with him if that is what you want."

"It would be no hardship," she said, "if he would like to."

—IRELAND, 8TH CENTURY

From *Mist*:

In Mist, *the great medieval Welsh poet Dafydd Ap Gwilym shows a sense of playfulness when addressing the Celtic view of open sexuality.*

Yesterday, Thursday, a day for drinking
(It was good for me to get) a gift came to me
(An omen of great import, I'm thin on her account),
A full love, I got
A session of sweet song under the greenwood
With a girl, she allows me to tryst.

—WALES, C. 1330–1360

From *The Wooing of Étain:*

In this selection from the Irish myth The Wooing of Étain, *the Dagda, the "good god," desires to sleep with Elcmar, another man's wife, and will do anything to have her. She also feels the same way about him. Here we see that although this story was probably first written down in the eighth century, it portrays women as having the same needs and desires as men.*

There was over Eriu a famous king from the Tuatha Dé Danann, and Echu Ollathir was his name. Another name for him was the Dagda, for it was he who performed miracles and saw to the weather and the harvest, and that is why he was called the Good God. Elcmar of Bruig na Boinde had a wife whose name was Eithne, though she was called Boand. The Dagda wanted to sleep with Boande, and she would have allowed him, but she feared Elcmar and the extent of his power. The Dagda sent Elcmar away, then, on a journey to Bress son of Elatha at Mag Ninis; and as Elcmar was leaving, the Dagda cast great spells upon him, so that he would not return quickly, so that he would not perceive the darkness of night, so that he would feel neither hunger nor thirst. The Dagda charged Elcmar with great commissions, so that nine months passed like a single day, for Elcmar had said that he would return before nightfall. The Dagda slept with Elcmar's wife, then, and she bore him a son, who was named Oenghus: and by the time of Elcmar's return, she has so recovered that he had no inkling of her having slept with the Dagda.

—IRELAND, 8TH CENTURY

Shape-Changing

I have been a blue salmon
I have been a wild dog,
I have been a cautious stag,
I have been a deer on the mountain
And a stump of a tree on a shovel
I have been an axe in the hand
A pin in a pair of tongs
A stallion in stud
A bull in anger
A grain in the growing
I have been dead,
I have been alive
I am a composer of songs
For I am Taliesin.
—The Welsh shape-shifting poet Taliesin, 6th century

The ability to transform oneself into a variety of guises is one of the most fascinating elements in Celtic storytelling. Ancient gods assumed a variety of forms, very often to elude their enemies or to visit the Otherworld. In war, many gods assumed the shape of boars in order to become more powerful in battle.

From *The Children of Llyr:*

In the ancient Celtic romance The Children of Llyr, *Eva, the quintessential evil stepmother, uses shape-changing as punish-*

ment. When her sister Eve dies, Eva marries Eve's husband, Llyr,
and raises his four children as her own. But these are no ordinary
children; they are beloved by all, particularly by their father, and
surpass all others in beauty and in goodness. Eva soon becomes
consumed with jealousy and turns Llyr's children into four white
swans.

Now when Eva saw that the children of Llyr received such
attention and affection from their father, and from all others that
came to house, she fancied she was neglected on their account;
and a poisonous dart of jealousy entered her heart, which turned
her love to hatred; and she began to have feelings of bitter enmity
for her sister's children.

Her jealousy so preyed on her that she feigned illness, and lay
in bed for nearly a year, filled with gall and brooding mischief; and
that the end of that time she committed a foul and cruel deed of
treachery on the children of Llyr.

One day she ordered her horses to be yoked to her chariot,
and she set out for the palaces of Bove Derg, bringing the four
children with her. Finola did not wish to go, for it was revealed to
her darkly in a dream that Eva was bent on some dreadful deed;
and she knew well that her stepmother intended to kill her and
her brothers that day, or in some other way to bring ruin on them.
But she was not able to avoid the fate that awaited her.

When they had gone some distance from Shee Finnaha on
their way to the palace, Eva tried to persuade her attendants to kill
the children. "Kill them, and you shall be rewarded with all the
worldly wealth you may desire; for their father loves me no longer,
and he has neglected and forsaken me on account of his great love
for these children."

But they heard her with horror, and refused, saying: "We will
not kill them. Fearful is the deed thou hast comtemplated, O Eva;

and evil shall surely befall thee for even having thought of killing them."

Then she took the sword to slay them herself; but her woman's weakness prevented her, and she was not able to strike them. So they set out once more, and fared on till they came to the shore of Lake Darva, where they alighted, and the horses were unyoked.

She led the children to the edge of the lake, and told them to go to bathe; and as soon as they had got into the clear water, she struck them one by one with a druidical fairy wand, and turned them into four beautiful snow-white swans. And she addressed them in these words:

Out to your home, ye swans, on Darva's wave;
With clamourous birds begin your life of gloom:
Your friends shall weep your fate, but none can save;
For I've pronounced the dreadful words of doom.

After this, the four children of Llyr turned their faces to their stepmother; and Finola spoke:

"Evil is the deed thou hast done, O Eva; thy friendship to us has been a friendship of treachery; and thou hast ruined us without cause. But the deed will be avenged; for the power of thy witchcraft is not greater than the druidical power of our friends to punish thee; and the doom that awaits you shall be worse than ours."

Our stepmother loved us long ago;
Our stepmother now has wrought us woe;
With magical wand and fearful words,
She changed us to beautiful snow-white birds;
And we live on the waters for evermore,
By tempests driven from shore to shore.

Finola again spoke and said: "Tell us now how long we shall be in the shape of swans, so that we may know when our miseries shall come to an end."

"It would be better for if you had not put that question," said Eva; "But I shall declare the truth to you, as you have asked me. Three hundred years on smooth Lake Darva; three hundred years on the Sea of Moyle, between Erin and Alban; three hundred years at Irros Domnann and at Inis Glora on the Western Sea. Until the union of Largnen, the prince from the north, with Decca, the princess from the south; until the Taillkenn shall come to Erin, bringing the light of a pure faith; and until ye hear the voice of the Christian bell. And neither by your own power, nor by mine, nor by the power of your friends, can ye be freed till the time comes."

—IRELAND, 8TH CENTURY

From *The Song of Amairgin:*

The ancient Irish poet Amairgin was thought to be the first Druid in Ireland. In this most famous poem from The Book of Invasions, *he declared that he could turn himself into all manner of animals.*

I am a wind on the sea;
I am a wave of the ocean;
I am the roar of the sea;
I am a powerful ox;
I am a hawk on a cliff;
I am a dewdrop in the sunshine;

I am a boar for valour;
I am a salmon in pools;
I am a lake in a plain;

I am the strength of art;
I am a spear with spoils that wages battle;
I am a man that shapes fire for a head.
Who clears the stone-place of the mountain?
What the place in which the setting of the sun lies?
Who has sought peace without fear seven times?
Who names the waterfalls?
Who brings his cattle from the house of Tethra?
What person, what god,
Forms weapons in a fort?
In a fort that nourishes satirists,
Chants a petition, divides the Ogam letters,
Separates a fleet, has sung praises?
A wise satirist.

—IRELAND, 8TH CENTURY

In this selection from The Mabinogion, *we see shape-shifting also used as a form of punishment. Here, King Arthur wages battle with his enemy, Twrch Trwyth, and only manages to kill one piglet, who used to be a king.*

Then Arthur collected all the warriors that were in Britain and the three offshore islands, in France, Brittany, Normandy and the Summer Country, along with selected dogs and renowned horses, and that entire army went to Ireland; at their coming there was fear and trembling in that island. When Arthur landed the saints of Ireland came to him seeking protection, and when he granted them that they gave him their blessing. The men of Ireland also came, bringing a gift of food. After that Arthur went to Ysgeir Oervel, where Twrch Trwyth and his seven young pigs were; from all sides dogs were unleashed at Twrch, and the Irish fought with him all day until evening, and at that he destroyed a fifth part of Ireland. The next day Arthur's troops fought with him, but except for the harm they suffered they got nothing; the third day Arthur himself fought with Twrch, nine days and nine nights, and killed nothing more than one piglet. His men asked him about the meaning of the pig and Arthur said, "He was a king, but because of his sins God turned him into a pig."

—WALES, 14TH CENTURY

From *The Dindschenchas:*

In ancient Irish myth, fairies were believed to have the power to steal humans away in the middle of the night and turn them into animals. In the poem Faffand *from* The Dindshenchas, *the collection of ancient Irish stories recalling how famous figures and places got their names, we see how the beautiful Aige was changed into the famous doe.*

Broccaid the powerful with winning of hostages,
Of the pure and famous race of the Galian,
He had a son, Faifne the poet;
Not false is the account of his final madness.

It was she was the mother of the comely son—
Even Libir quick and eager of mood:
Their daughter was the swift lady of the hosts
Aige, the noble and skillful.

Exceeding fair were the four, curled and gentle;
They were a noble kin, of virtuous behaviour.
The daughter and the mother were lovely,
The father and the son of great beauty.
The spirits of the faery caught them,
(Not feeble the deed . . . .);

They changed into the form of a wild doe
The noble Aige of the love spots.

She traversed Erin from shore to shore
[Fleeing] before all the red and fiery packs;
So that she coursed round Banba, land of judges,
Bravely in the form of a fair beast.

—IRELAND, C. A.D. 1150

War

The most common image of the ancient Celt remains that of
the bloodthirsty soldier who lives for war. This stereotype is not
entirely unwarranted. The ancient Celts were renowned for their
warrior skills, and much of their literature reflects this all-consuming
passion for winning in battle. Ancient Irish societies were ruled by
a warrior class whose purpose was to defend and enrich the life of
the whole tribe. Boys were taught battle skills at the age of fourteen, most often by women. Weapons of war also took on a magical property and were thought to provide supernatural power to
those who used them.

From *The Táin:*

*The Táin is rife with references to war and the qualities that a
great warrior must possess. To this day its hero, Cuchulainn, remains the epitome of the Celtic warrior—brave, honorable, and
preternaturally strong.*

195

"It's a poor sort of warrior that lies down at the feet of a ghost."

—IRELAND, 8TH CENTURY, CUCHULAINN,
FROM *CUCHULAINN'S BOYHOOD DEEDS*

"I swear by my gods," said Cuchulain, "that until they in turn come under my protection and guarantee I will not lighten my hand from off them.

—IRELAND, 8TH CENTURY, CUCHULAINN,
FROM *CUCHULAINN'S BOYHOOD DEEDS*

"It will be easier on us, no doubt . . . to lose one man every day than a hundred every night."

—IRELAND, 8TH CENTURY, AILILL,
FROM *SINGLE COMBAT*

"I have held them single-handed,
But one stone won't make fire.
Give me two or three
And torches will blaze!"

—IRELAND, 8TH CENTURY, CUCHULAINN,
FROM *HEALING OF THE MORRIGAN*

"A warrior without his weapons is not under warriors' law; he is treated under the rule for cowards."

—IRELAND, 8TH CENTURY, LAEG THE CHARIOTEER,
FROM *THE PACT IS BROKEN: THE GREAT CARNAGE*

"My skill in arms grows great.
On fine armies cowering
I let fall famous blows.
On whole hosts I wage war
To crush their chief hero

And Medb and Ailill also
Who stir up wrong, red hatred
And black woman-wailing,
Who march in cruel treachery
Trampling their chief hero
And his sage, sound advice
—a fierce right speaking warrior
Full of noble acts."

    —IRELAND, 8TH CENTURY, CUCHULAINN,
      FROM *THE PACT IS BROKEN: THE GREAT CARNAGE*

"Here stands one to crush thee,
'Tis I will destroy thee
From me there shall come
The flight of their warriors
In presence of Ulster
That long they'll remember
The loss that was theirs!"

    —IRELAND, 8TH CENTURY, FERDIAD,
      FROM *THE COMBAT OF FERDIAD AND CUCHULAINN*

"O' Cuchulain—wise decree—
Loyal champion, hero true
Each man is constrained to go
'Neath the sod that hides his grace!"

    —IRELAND, 8TH CENTURY, FERDIAD,
      FROM *THE COMBAT OF FERDIAD AND CUCHULAINN*

In this selection from The Mabinogion, *Kynon and Maxen devise a clever plan to defeat the Romans.*

There had followed Maxen from the island of Britain a small band led by the brothers of Elen of the Hosts, and there were better fighters in that small band than among twice as many Romans. The emperor was told how this band had been seen dismounting and pitching their tents near his own, and how no one had ever seen a finer band nor one better equipped, nor with handsomer standards for their size. Elen of the Hosts went to look, and she recognized the standards of her brothers; thus Kynon and Avaon came to see Maxen, and he threw his arms about them and welcomed them. They all went to look at the Roman assault on the stronghold, and Kynon said to his brother, "We should look for a cleverer way to take this stronghold." At night they measured the height of the wall, and then they sent their carpenters into the forest and had a ladder made for every four men, and soon the ladders were ready. Every day at noon the two emperors would stop fighting and eat their meal. The British, however, took their food and drink in the morning, until they were in high spirits, and so when the two emperors were eating the British approached the wall and set their ladders against it, and at once they scaled the wall and dropped over inside. The new emperor had no opportunity to arm himself before they were upon him; they killed him and many others, and three days and nights they spent overcoming the host in the fortress and in conquering the castle, while another part of them were on watch lest any of Maxen's host should enter before they had finished. Maxen said to Elen of the Hosts, "Lady, I marvel greatly that it is not for me that your brothers have conquered this fortress," and she answered, "Lord, my brothers are the wisest men in the world. Go and ask for the stronghold, and if they control it they will gladly give it to you." So Maxen and Elen went to ask for the fortress, and Maxen was told that its capture and surrender to him was the doing of none save the men of the island of Britain. The gate to the fortress of Rome was then opened, and the emperor sat in his chair and the Romans did him homage.

—WALES, 14TH CENTURY

Work

The ancient Celts took exceptional pride in their work, specifically in learning skilled trades. Excellence in craftsmanship was a great part of one's self-esteem, and exalted his position in the tribe. The Brehon Laws include smiths in the ranking of the highest members of Irish society, and many of the provisions in the laws judge a person's worth by the kind of work they engage in. As a result, the Celts' skill in gold, silver, bronze, and ironworks proved to be particularly miraculous. As T. G. E. Powell asserts in *The Celts*, "It was perhaps the very diversity of their environment and material resources, together with their lively disposition, and the elasticity of their social structure within the free grades, that brought to the Celts a standard of achievement in arts and crafts unparalleled among the ancient inhabitants of trans-alpine Europe."

This passion for work is especially apparent in the Welsh literature, particularly in the story of Manawydan son of Llyr, in which the hero takes his men to England to seek employment. Their total devotion to being the best in their trade ensures their excellence in every job they undertake, but it also causes the envy of the other tradesman that they compete with. In this same way, we also see the importance of work in the writings of the monastic saints, who saw engaging in hard and purposeful work as a path to holiness.

From *The Senchus Mor:*

Every man is a saer person who purchases his freedom [i.e. nobility] by his art such as the smith. For the smith, if he has made the tool [or structure], for each neighbour of the four neighbourhoods that are around him, through which screpalls of free offering come to him—[or though he has not done so if he has not accepted] is free from the crime of his food and from the crime of his kinsman; and dire fine and honour price are due for stealing his tools.

—IRELAND, C. A.D. 438

From *The Senchus Mor:*

Every art, therefore, that we have named, which is entitled to nobility, does not lose the nobility to which it is entitled in a territory by a man's not practising his art, if he holds [property], whether it be in a territory or in a church he be. It is hence it is said "Not unless Nemeds diminish." He who has one art, let him have one dire; he who has many, let him have many dires: it increases nobility.

Musicians and sportmakers in general, viz. equestrians and chariot-drivers, pilots and conjurers and companies and scarifiers and jugglers and buffoons and podicinists, and all mean arts in like manner: it is on account of the person with whom they are, it is out of him they are paid; there is no nobility for them severally at all.

—IRELAND, C. A.D. 438

From *Adiutor laborantium:*

The poem Adiutor laborantium, *which was composed by St. Columba as he was grinding corn in the mill at his monastery, pays homage to the belief that hard work was a form of praising God.*

O helper of workers,
Ruler of all the good,
Guard on the ramparts
And defender of the faithful,
Who lift up the lowly
And crush the proud,
Ruler of the faithful,
Enemy of the impenitent,
Judge of all judges,
Who punish those who err,
Pure life of the living,
Light and Father of lights
Shining with great light,
Denying to none of the hopeful
Your strength and help,
I beg that me, a little man,
Trembling and most wretched,
Rowing through the infinite storm
Of this age,
Christ may draw after him to the lofty
Most beautiful haven of life
. . . and unending
Holy hymn forever.
From the envy of enemies you lead me
Into the joy of paradise.
Through you, Christ Jesus,
Who live and reign. . . .

—IRELAND, C. A.D. 512

In this selection, Manawydan and Pryderi set off to England to work, and in true Celtic fashion, they excel at everything they do, thereby gaining the scorn of everyone they compete with.

"Let us go to England to seek a trade by which we can support ourselves." So they set out for England, and when they had settled in Hereford, they took up saddlemaking. Manawydan shaped and coloured the pommels as he had seen Llassar Llaes Gyngwyd do with blue enamel; he made this enamel exactly as Llassar had done, and for this reason it is still called calch llassar—because Llassar Llaes Gyngwyd made it. As for the work, so long as a saddle or pommel could be got from Manawydan it would not be bought from any other saddler in Hereford. When these other saddlers realized that they were selling only what Manawydan could not supply they formed a conspiracy and decided to kill their rival and his companion; the strangers received a warning, however, and they in turn held a council to decide whether they should leave town. "Between me and God, I do not think we ought to leave—better to kill these churls," said Pryderi, but Manawydan answered, "No, for if we fought with them, we should earn a bad reputation, and be thrown into prison. Better for us to seek another town and earn our living there."

The four made for another city. "What trade shall we take up here?" asked Pryderi. "We will make shields," said Manawydan. "Do we know anything about shieldmaking?" "We will try it," Manawydan answered. They began to make shields, shaping them to resemble the good ones they had seen and colouring them as they had coloured the saddles. Their work prospered so that no shield was bought elsewhere in the town unless it could not be had from them. They worked swiftly and made countless shields, and this went on until their competitors became angry and conspired to kill them; however, they were told of these plans. "Pryderi, these men want to kill us," said Manawydan. "We ought not to take that from the rascals. Let us go and kill them," said Pryderi, but Manawydan answered, "No, for Casswallawn and his

men would hear of it, and then we should come to grief. Let us go
to another town."

They did that and Manawydan said, "What craft shall we
take up here?" "Whichever one you prefer of the two we know,"
said Pryderi, but Manawydan answered, "No, we should take to
shoemaking, for shoemakers are not bold enough to kill us or for-
bid our working." "I know nothing of that trade," said Pryderi.
"Well, I do," said Manawydan, "and I will show you how to stitch.
We will not bother to tan the leather; instead we will buy it already dressed and work from that." They bought the best cordovan that was to be had in the town, for everything except the
soles. Manawydan visited the best goldsmith in town; he had the
latter make gilded buckles for the shoes, and moreover he
watched until he knew how to do the gilding himself—for that
reason he was called one of the Three Golden Shoemakers. So as
long as a shoe or boot could be had from him it would not be
bought from any other shoemaker in town, and his competitors
perceived they were losing business, for Pryderi stitched the shoes
as expertly as Manawydan cut them out. "Pryderi, the shoemakers
are planning to kill us," said Manawydan. "Why should we take
that from the thieving churls and not kill them?" asked Pryderi,
but Manawydan answered, "No, we will not fight them, nor will
we remain here. Let us return to Dyved."

—WALES, FROM *MANAWYDAN SON OF LLYR*

From *The Plowman:*

*This ode to the working man by the Welsh Poet Iolo Goch (c.
1325–1398) also confirms the Celtic belief that hard work put
one on the path to God.*

When all the world's people show,
Christendom's fine host, their deeds

Before God at some free time,
Good bold words, eager desire,
On top of the mighty Mount
Of Olives, place of judgment,
Joyful will be the sure speech
Of the plowman, field-farer,
If he gave freely to God
An offering and his tithe, a good soul then to God
Will he pay, earning reward.
The plowman can happily
Trust in God after this life;
He always gives to all men
Good charity and shelter;
He judges only the plowbeam,
He hates ire among his fellows;
He doesn't wage war or harrass,
He doesn't rob a man by force;
He is never harsh to us,
He makes no claim, forbearing fault;
Not fitting, by the passion,
No life, no world without him.
I know he would far rather,
Placid unchanging manner,
Follow, I'm glad, with no blame,
The crooked plow with the goad
Than be Arthur the ravager
Demolishing a tower.
Without his work we wouldn't have
Christ's body to feed the world,
Nor could pope nor emperor
Live without him—why find fault?—
Nor fine-wine dispensing king,
Sure his sense, nor any man.

Good old Lucidarius
Made this sure pronouncement:
Blessed, against pain beyond,
Is he who handles the plow.

—WALES, C. A.D. 1398

BIBLIOGRAPHY

Barbour, John. *The Bruce*. Glasgow: William MacClellan, 1964.

Bede. *Opera Historica: Books 1–3*. London: Willian Heinemann, Ltd., 1930.

Bryant, Sophie, D.Sc., Litt.D. *Liberty, Order, & Law: Under Native Irish Rule*. New York: Encyclopedia Press, 1923.

Butler, Isabel, trans. *Tales from the Old French*. Boston and New York: Houghton Mifflin Co., 1910.

Caesar, Julius. *The Conquest of Gaul*. New York, Penguin Books, 1982.

———. *The Gallic War*. Cambridge: Harvard University Press, 1917.

Carey, John. *King of Mysteries: Early Irish Religious Writing*. Dublin: Four Courts Press, 1998.

Clancy, Thomas Owen and Markus, Gilbert. *Iona: The Earliest Poetry of a Celtic Monastery*. Edinburgh: Edinburgh University Press, 1995.

Comfort, W. Wistar, trans. *Arthurian Romances by Chrétien de Troyes*. London and Toronto: J.M. Dent and Sons, Ltd., 1914.

Cunliffe, Barry. *The Ancient Celts*. New York: Penguin Books, 1999.

Curtin, Jeremiah, ed. *Hero Tales of Ireland*. New York: Benjamin Blom, 1894.

DeVere, Aubrey. *The Legends of St. Patrick*. London: Henry S. King & Co., 1872.

Dunn, Joseph. *The Ancient Irish Epic Tale Táin Bó Cúalnge*. London: David Nutt, 1914.

Ellis, T.P., M.A., and Lloyd, John, trans. *The Mabinogion*. Oxford: Clarendon Press, 1929.

Ellis, Peter Beresford. *The Celtic Empire*. New York: Caroll & Graf Publishers, 1996.

Glynn, Edward, M.A., trans. *Poems from The Dindshenchas*. Dublin: Royal Irish Academy, 1900.

Gregory, Lady Augusta, trans. *Cuchulain of Muirthemne*. New York: Charles Scribner's Sons, 1903.

Halliday, F.E. *The Legend of the Rood*. London: Gerald Duckworth & Co., Ltd., 1955.

Hennessy, William, ed. *Annals of Ulster Vol.1: A Chronicle of Irish Affairs A.D. 431–1056*. Dublin: Alex. Thom & Co., 1893.

Herodotus. *The Histories*. New York: Penguin Books, 1972.

Hood, A.B.E., trans. *St. Patrick: His Writings and Muirchu's Life*. London: Phillimore & Co., Ltd., 1978.

Jackson, Kenneth H. *Studies in Early Celtic Nature Poetry*. Cambridge: Cambridge University Press, 1935.

———. *The Gododdin*. Edinburgh: Edinburgh University Press, 1969.

———. *Early Welsh Gnomic Poems*. Cardiff: The University of Wales Press, 1935.

Joyce, P.W. *Old Celtic Romances: Tales from Irish Mythology*. London: David Nutt, 1894.

Knott, E., ed. *The Bardic Poems of Tadhg Dall O'Huiginn*. Lundain: Irish Texts Society, 1921.

Leslie, Shane. *Saint Patrick's Purgatory*. London: Burns, Oates & Washbourne, Ltd., 1932.

Loomis, Richard and Johnston, Dafydd. *Medieval Welsh Poems*. Binghampton: Medieveal and Renaissance Texts & Studies, 1992.

MacCarthy, B., D.D., MRIA, ed. *Annals of Ulster Vol. II: A Chronicle of Irish Affairs A.D. 1057–1131*. Dublin: Alex. Thom & Co, 1893.

MacClean, Magnus. *The Literature of the Highlands*. London: Blackie & Son, Ltd., 1904.

MacKillop, James. *The Dictionary of Celtic Mythology.* Oxford: Oxford University Press, 1998.

Matthews, John. *The Song of Taliesin.* London: Unwin Hyman, 1991.

McLaughlin, Rev. Thomas, trans. *The Dean of Lismore's Book: A Selection of Ancient Gaelic Poetry.* Edinburgh: Edmonston and Douglas, 1862.

Meyer, Kuno and Nutt, Alfred. *The Voyage of Bran.* London: David Nutt in the Strand, 1895.

Neeson, Eoin. *The First Book of Irish Myths and Legends.* Cork: The Mercier Press, 1965.

Newell, Willian Wells, ed. *King Arthur and the Table Round: Tales Chiefly after the Old French of Chrestien of Troyes.* New York: Houghton Mifflin and Co., 1897.

Rofle, John C., trans. *Marcellinus Ammianus: Book 1.* Cambridge: Harvard University Press, 1935.

Rolleston, T.W. *Myths and Legends of the Celtic Race.* London: George G. Harrap & Co., 1911.

Shuckburg, Evelyn, trans. *The Histories of Polybius.* London: Mac-Millan and Co., 1889.

Wheatley, Henry B., ed. *Merlin, or The Early History of King Arthur: A Prose Romance (1450–1460 A.D.).* London: The Early English Text Society, 1899.

ABOUT THE EDITORS

DR. PATRICIA KING holds a Ph.D. in Irish Studies, and was formerly Director of Ireland House, the Center for Irish Studies and culture at New York University. She was also a founding Director of NYU's Tisch School of the Arts Dublin program, and a cofounder of the Irish Arts Center in New York. She received her B.A. from Marymount College; her M.A. from Notre Dame University; and she did postgraduate study at Trinity College, Dublin and received her Ph.D. in Irish Studies from the Graduate Center of CUNY. She is currently on leave and living with her family in Connecticut.

GINA SIGILLITO has studied Celtic mythology, art, philosophy, and Christianity since 1990 at a variety of schools including the Irish Arts Center, Ireland House at New York University, and Trinity College, Dublin. She attended Columbia and Fordham Universities in New York City and holds a B.A. in English and journalism. She has contributed to a variety of publications including the *Irish People Newspaper, Saoirse,* and *Carn.* From 1997–2000, she served as a guest host and producer on the Irish radio program "Radio Free Éireann" on WBAI-FM 99.5 in New York City. She has lectured in New York City on women in Irish history at a number of venues including the Irish Arts Center, New York's City Hall, Fordham University, and Hunter College, and has traveled extensively throughout Ireland.

Síle Deady teaches a course in Irish art and architecture at the Irish Arts Center in New York City. She holds a B.A. in archeology and has excavated at sites ranging from the Neolithic at Newgrange, Ireland, to Viking sites in the Hebrides of Scotland. She also holds a degree in art and architectural history and lived in Rome from 1990–1994, where she taught Rococo art and architecture. She has worked as a researcher for the National Gallery of Art and with Fingal County Council, both in Dublin, Ireland, advising on buildings of historic and architectural interest. She has lectured on Celtic art at a variety of venues including the United Nations, and wrote Ireland's art catalog entry for the Millennium Exhibition.